D0464920

The Effect of Research and Development
on U.S. Market Structure

Research in Business Economics and Public Policy, No. 9

Fred Bateman, Series Editor

Chairman and Professor
Business Economics and Public Policy
Indiana University

Other Titles in This Series

The Effect of Research and Development on U.S. Market Structure

by
Edward M. Scahill, Jr.

UMI RESEARCH PRESS

Ann Arbor, Michigan

Produced and distributed by
UMI Research Press
an imprint of
University Microfilms International
A Xerox Information Resources Company
Ann Arbor, Michigan 48106

Library of Congress Cataloging in Publication Data

Scahill, Edward M., 1951-
  The effect of research and development on U.S.
market structure.

  (Research in business economics and public
policy ; no. 9)
  Revision of thesis (Ph.D.)—State University
of New York (SUNY) at Binghamton, 1983.
  Bibliography: p.
  Includes index.
  1. Industrial productivity—United States.
  2. Industrial concentration—United States.
  3. Research, Industrial—United States. I. Title.
  II. Series.
  HC79.I52S24   1985   338.0973   85-14118
  ISBN 0-8357-1691-0 (alk. paper)

To Anna and Michael Dominic

Contents

List of Tables

Acknowledgments

Many people have contributed, directly and indirectly, to the completion of this book. The first debt of gratitude that I owe is to Professor Frank Colella, who taught and counseled me during my undergraduate days at Saint Bonaventure University. For better or worse, my decision to pursue economics as a field of study was based primarily on my contact with him.

The members of my dissertation committee gave me valuable assistance and encouragement. Special thanks go to Professor Ronald Britto, the committee chairman, who spent much of his time and effort helping me through what was at times a frustrating endeavor. Professor Phillip Nelson directed me to several useful sources of information. Professor Bertrand Horwitz made valuable comments to me as an outside reader. The final member of my committee was Professor Jan Michal, with whom I spent a memorable year in Malta and Tunisia as an assistant to an overseas study program for which he was the field director. For that year he was both mentor and surrogate father to me.

My greatest obligations are to my wife and parents. My mother and father never failed to give me the encouragement and support I needed to pursue this and so many other projects. My wife, Anna, displayed infinite patience and understanding throughout the years spent on this work. Marrying Anna has been the ultimate example of "utility maximization."

Finally, I would like to thank Joanne Haag for her excellent job of typing, often under the pressure of impending deadlines.

1

The Economics of Research and Technological Change

There can be no doubt of the importance of the role that technological change plays in the growth of a nation's productivity. In a well-known study, Robert Solow estimated that about $87\frac{1}{2}$ percent of the increase in gross output per man-hour in the United States from 1909 to 1949 was attributable to technological change (where the latter term was understood to include improvements in the quality of the labor force, or the stock of capital, or any kind of shift in the production function).[1] Still other studies have noted that improvements in technology are often the result of successful investments by private firms (though financing may come from either private or government sources) in research and development (R and D). In examining the importance of R and D to America's pattern of international trade and investment, Gruber, and Mehta, and Vernon also noted that

> the industries with the strongest research effort are also those with the strongest new-product orientation. . . . To a considerable extent . . . high technical effort at any stage of the design-production-marketing process is associated with high technical effort at all the other stages . . . the intensity of the research and development effort is greatest in industries in which the degree of employment concentration is high, and in which large firms are particularly dominant . . . the statistics [indicate] that the large-scale high-concentration pattern is not associated with high capital intensity. . . . These findings suggest the existence of national markets in which economies of large scale and barriers to entry stem from the requirements of successful marketing rather than from capital intensity.[2]

It is interesting to note that studies like Solow's (concerned with the issues of economic growth and aggregate production functions) were inspired, at least in part, by the lack of an adequate explanation for the long-run growth of productivity. The study by Gruber, et al., was one of many that examined the contribution of R and D and technological change to the theory of international trade. Many of these latter works noted the apparent inability of the Hecksher-Ohlin factor proportions theory to explain the pattern of trade of the United States. The Hecksher-Ohlin theorem argues that a nation will have a comparative advantage in producing and exporting those products that use relatively large amounts of the nation's relatively abundant factor of production. Leontief's famous paradox seemed to contradict the conventional wisdom that the United States had its comparative advantage in producing capital-intensive manufactures.[3]

The economic analysis of R and D and technological change has a rather brief history. Neoclassical production functions typically have assumed that the output of a product depends upon the amounts of capital, labor, and other resources devoted to production, holding technology constant. The optimal combination of resources used by producers is then assumed to be determined by relative factor prices. The further assumption of perfect competition in factor and product markets enables one to treat prices as given parameters. Though the production function is a very useful tool of analysis for short-run or static production environments (as illustrated by the Hecksher-Ohlin theorem), the assumption of a "given state of technology" effectively placed technology outside of the realm of economic analysis. As Kamien and Schwartz have written:

> The objective of resource allocation appears to be . . . to make the best of available resources. The alternative objective of relaxing constraints through expanding the resource base or developing new technology seems to be beyond its scope. Thus, until rather recently, technical advance had been regarded, in the mainstream of economic theory, as unmotivated by the quest for profits and unaffected by resource allocation.[4]

The conventional analysis, then, treated technological change much like "manna from heaven": the result of chance discovery or the product of basic research (e.g., conducted in a university setting without any intention of developing a commercially successful product). The further assumption of perfect competition is consistent with this view of technology since competitive firms that produce a homogeneous product would have little incentive to risk devoting part of their resources to the development of a new process. Should the research fail, an innovating firm would be at a cost disadvantage with respect to its rivals; if successful, the new process would quickly be copied by other firms that would not have to incur the costs and risks of this research.

However, the evidence of the link between privately financed R and D and technological change has cast considerable doubt on the usefulness of the assumptions of perfect competition and "given technology." The results of studies show that "despite methodological difficulties and debates . . . the evidence—at the level of the firm, industry and the economy—indicates that the contribution of R and D to . . . productivity is positive, significant and high."[5]

Certainly, one of the most significant economic developments of the post-World War II era has been rapid growth of multinational corporations (MNCs), especially those whose headquarters are in the United States. The success that these relatively large firms have had, and the tendency for them to engage in R and D, as Gruber, Mehta, and Vernon found, emphasize the inadequacy of the assumption of perfect competition in a production function that purports to explain output growth. In a number of microeconomic studies, Edwin Mansfield and his colleagues have found that a great deal of uncertainty surrounds the effort by private firms to develop new technologies and that R and D is often a costly, time-consuming endeavor.[6] They also found that firms within the same industries often differ greatly in the types of technologies they develop and use.

It is useful to think of MNCs and other R and D intensive firms as specialists in the production of "technology" (or knowledge or information; these terms will be used interchangeably) which is embedded in new products or processes. The positive correlation between industry concentration, and large firm size, and research intensity may be due to the low appropriability of the returns to R and D in atomistic markets and the greater ability of large firms to absorb the costs that the uncertainty of R and D imposes. At the same time, successful innovation is likely to spur market growth and cause, ceteris paribus, industry structure to become more concentrated. New technology that is the result of private research efforts requires the use of scarce resources; once developed, however, the technology takes on the characteristics of a public good, in that noninnovating firms may acquire the technology without incurring the innovator's search costs. From a (short-run) social welfare standpoint the free dissemination of new knowledge is desirable; but unless the research is undertaken or sponsored by government, this would reduce the incentive that private firms have to engage in future research. Since investments in the development of technology are costly, innovating firms seek returns on their investments just as they would on their investments in plants and equipment. Innovating firms realize that the returns to their efforts are affected by their ability to prevent other firms from copying their successes, and this realization will influence the types of research that are undertaken.

In his analysis of the research activities of MNCs, Stephen Magee developed an "appropriability theory" of the creation of new knowledge:

> By "appropriability," we mean the ability of private originators of ideas to obtain for themselves the values of the ideas to society. The appropriability theory asserts that multinational corporate development is guided by careful calculations of the likelihood of loss of the returns on new information to emulators.[7]

MNCs use various devices designed to impede the use of new knowledge by others, e.g., patent protection; emphasis on development of sophisticated, hard-to-copy technology; and trade secrets. The research efforts of MNCs tend to be concentrated on product development rather than basic research. Expenditures are required for skilled personnel (scientists, engineers, and managers) who conduct applied research and engage in product or process specification and modification. Pilot plants must be established, test marketing undertaken, and startup costs incurred. Mansfield has noted that it can take five to ten years for a major product to be developed.[8] Obviously, this is an expensive undertaking, especially since not all research projects are commercially successful and the payments for skilled labor are typically fixed costs. Certainly, relatively large firms are better able to afford the costs of product development; but this also implies that innovators will seek to sell their products in the broadest possible markets in order to maximize the returns from their investments. Increasingly, these markets have reached across national boundaries. For example, data for 1978 show that for 150 large United States corporations, 37 percent of their revenue came from foreign markets.[9] Consider these comments from corporate executives:

> Our research and development expenditure is so great the only way you can get a proper return is to go for a very big market. And no single market—not even the U.S.—can really do the job of giving us a good return.
> —Dow Chemical Chairman
>   Paul Oreffice

> In terms of the amount that comes in for a dollar, you could say it was more profitable to invest overseas.
> —Standard Oil of California
>   Vice President, Planning
>   Dennis Bonney

> For a company which already has realized a good share of its potential in the U.S. market, or a less mature company which has discovered an outstanding new product that will attract strong demand elsewhere, then the case for worldwide marketing seems almost irresistible.
> —CEO for Pfizer
>   John Powers[10]

Furthermore, Mansfield, Romeo, and Wagner have shown, in a survey of 30 MNCs, the importance of foreign markets to the research effort of these firms.[11] They noted that as much as a 26 percent reduction in R and D expenditures could be expected if these firms were unable to utilize their technology in foreign markets.

Successful innovation brings with it relatively rapid sales growth and high profits, which tend to expand firm size, and often, industry concentration. The development of the drug Tagamet by the SmithKline Corporation offers a textbook example of the risks, costs, and potential rewards of new product development.[12] Tagamet went on sale in November 1976 as a cure for peptic ulcers. The drug allows ulcers to heal by blocking the formation of hydrochloric acid in the stomach. The subsequent success that Tagamet found in the marketplace has made it one of the most successful product innovations in U. S. business history. By 1979 SmithKline's revenues had increased by 129 percent over their 1975 level, and its profits had increased by 266 percent over the same period. Tagamet had accounted for more than one-third of the company's 1979 revenues and almost one-half of its profits. SmithKline, long a laggard among other pharmaceutical companies in its pre-Tagamet days, was transformed practically overnight into one of the most successful firms on Wall Street, with its stock's price soaring from a low of $10.81 in 1975 to $65.25 in 1979 (by which time there had been two stock splits).

However, the success of Tagamet came only after a long trial and error process that had almost led SmithKline's management to abandon the search for an ulcer cure altogether.

The quest for what came to be known as Tagamet had been going on since 1964 at the SmithKline lab in Welwyn Garden City, England. "They had drilled a million dry holes," says one SmithKline officer. The researchers had synthesized 700 different compounds, seeking a formula that would block the production by histamine of hydrochloric acid in the gastrointestinal tract. . . . Late in 1969 Thomas M. Rauch, then SmithKline's chief executive, gave an ultimatum: come up with something in one year or see the program die.[13]

By 1970 researchers had made enough progress to salvage the program, and by 1971 they had finally developed a drug that could be taken orally. Though successful, the drug produced side effects that called for further modification. Finally, in 1976 in Great Britain and in 1977 in the United States, SmithKline was given permission to sell Tagamet to the general public. Even then, company officials underestimated the demand for the product since there was no way to estimate the demand for the product among those who were treating ulcer symptoms with their own diets and over-the-counter antacids.

A corollary to Magee's appropriability theory is that MNCs will transfer new technology to foreign markets through the vehicle that maximizes the returns to their investments. Generally, the innovator may choose to transfer technology through one of the following vehicles: (a) majority-owned subsidiary (the parent firm owns over 50 percent of the equity of the affiliate); (b) minority-owned joint venture (equity ownership is less than 50 percent); (c) licensing (the rights to the technology are sold to an independent firm); (d) exporting. Many factors influence the choice of vehicle. Magee claims that, for many new products and processes, appropriability is greatest when transfer is effected through a majority-owned subsidiary.

One may note that Magee's analysis is consistent with the industrial organization approach to foreign direct investment that was pioneered by Stephen Hymer and Richard Caves.[14] Both men argued that such investments were commonly undertaken by large firms in oligopolistic industries. Caves' work emphasized that since national firms in foreign markets have inherent advantages vis-a-vis the MNC (e.g., greater familiarity with market conditions and, possibly, favored treatment from their governments), the successful investor must possess some "unique asset," so that it can differentiate its product. Caves claimed, however, that any advantage obtained by the MNC will be temporary. It was in this context that Vernon wrote:

When any [MNC] . . . decides to set up a producing subsidiary in a given market, others are disposed to look more favorably on creating a similar subsidiary in the same market. . . .
. . . the leaders in industries that produce standardized products are concerned about the heavy fixed costs they are obliged to bear; these costs stem partly from the production process, but

they may also arise from the need to maintain an organization and a distribution system. A dominant risk, as the leaders see it, is that others in the same product line may build up their sales,
reduce their unit costs, and overrun their competition.[15]

Magee makes use of this idea by invoking once again the appropriability theory:
over time the returns to a new product or process will diminish if emulators attempt to follow into the innovator's market. This will cause changes in the degree
of concentration in the foreign market. Thought relevant data are hard to come
by, there is some support for Magee's hypothesis that, especially for relatively
new products and processes, MNCs prefer transfer via majority-owned subsidiary,
but that this preference wanes as the product or process ages.

The association that has been made between research and market structure
can be related to the studies that have examined the relationship between market
structure and industry profits across United States industries. Many studies have
found industry concentration and profits to be positively related, although the
strength of this relationship is the subject of some disagreement[16] (e.g., Yale Brozen
has been especially critical of the majority of these studies).[17] Certainly, one possible
explanation for this relationship is that oligopolistic firms may find it easier to
collude (or, at least, not to compete aggressively through their pricing policies),
so that above-normal profits are the result of relatively high prices. An alternative
explanation was offered by Demsetz, who argued that high profits might be the
reward given to the most efficient producers. For example, if a firm in a given
industry produced the proverbial widget at a lower cost than its rivals, it would
increase its market share. Industry unit costs would decline since the most efficient firm would sell more, and the industry would experience an increase in concentration. The most efficient firm(s) could earn relatively high profits without
necessarily charging collusive prices.

Demsetz tested his hypothesis by examining four-firm concentration ratios
and accounting rates of return of U.S. industries for 1963, 1969, and 1970.[18] He
was able to break down the profit figures by firm size and found that: (1) the largest
firms in high-concentration industries had profit rates that were significantly higher
than other firms in the same industry, (2) the largest firms in low-concentration
industries had profit rates that were not significantly different from other firms
in the same industries. Demsetz argued that if the superior profit performance
were the result of collusion, small firms not engaged in price-fixing would benefit
from the "price umbrella" erected by the colluding firms. Since he found that
it was only in high-concentration industries (where the possibilities for successful
collusion should be the greatest) that smaller firms earned low rates of return,
Demsetz reasoned that large firms were more efficient in these industries due to
gains from economies of scale, technological or managerial superiority, etc. In
general, the large firms had lower average costs than smaller rivals. Since the gains
due to scale economies would be minimal in low-concentration industries, one

would expect there to be less of a difference between the profit rates of large and small firms. Therefore, Demsetz concluded that his empirical results vindicated his hypothesis.

Peltzman further examined the relationship between industry unit costs and concentration.[19] He noted that Demsetz' results could be consistent with a number of possible outcomes; e.g., more efficient large firms could still engage in collusion. The superior profit performance would then result from both causes, with the relative contribution of each not clearly ascertainable. Peltzman constructed a mathematical model which related unit cost changes for two groups of industries: those that experienced increased concentration from 1947 to 1967 and those whose concentration had decreased. Peltzman found that an increase in concentration in a nongrowing market resulted in no significant change in costs, while in rapidly growing markets there was a statistically significant decline in unit costs among the industries in the increased concentration subsample. Decreases in concentration were associated with reduced costs, but the size of this effect was small and statistically insignificant.

Though Peltzman's results provided some support for Demsetz' view, his model was criticized by Lustgarten, who noted some irregularities in the results.[20] Especially critical was the fact that the results depended on an interaction between market growth and the change in concentration. It was not possible to infer what the independent effect of each variable on unit costs was. In a revision of Peltzman's regression equation, Lustgarten estimated the relationship between unit cost changes and market structure variables for 159 four-digit SIC industries (data were for 1954-1972). Again, separate estimates were obtained for the two subsamples of industries (those with decreased and increased concentration for the sample period); and he found that increased concentration was (significantly) negatively related to cost changes when only the direct effect was estimated. Increased concentration was (significantly) positively related to unit cost changes.

Another criticism of Peltzman's work was leveled by Scherer.[21] Though he conceded that cost reductions have accompanied increases in industry concentration, he questioned whether this was due to discoveries of cost-reducing innovations, as Peltzman suggested. Technological change in many industries since World War II, he noted, has been in the form of product, not process, innovation. These studies emphasize how difficult it is to attribute changes in costs or productivity to specific causes. Still, the hypothesized relationship between industry concentration and efficiency suggested by Demsetz and Peltzman is an interesting one, with clear policy implications (especially with respect to antitrust).

The remainder of this study will investigate the issues presented above in greater detail. In particular, the study reviews the roles that R and D, technological change, and market structure play in the theories of international trade and investment. It then covers issues related to the study of concentration and efficiency in more detail. Some of the theoretical and empirical difficulties involved in measuring the effects of R and D on changes in costs and productivity are reviewed. Finally, the study presents estimates of the effects of R and D and other variables on productivity growth for recent time periods.

2

Research and Development, Technological Change, and Foreign Trade and Investment

Since World War II many economists have examined the role that research and development has played in influencing the pattern of international trade and investment. Traditionally, the Hecksher-Ohlin factor proportions theory of trade has been used to explain the pattern of comparative advantage across nations. Briefly stated, this theory argues that a country (in a model with two goods and two factors of production) would find its comparative advantage in (and hence would export) that good whose production process used relatively large amounts of the factor that was relatively abundant within the country. Though the factor proportions explanation is still the most fundamental trade theory, new approaches were explored subsequent to the publication of one of the most famous of all empirical studies, the so-called Leontief paradox.[1] Leontief's findings seemed to contradict what the then conventional wisdom had suggested: the United States, certainly a country rich in capital, would find its comparative advantage in producing products whose production required relatively large amounts of capital. Instead, Leontief found that U.S. exports were more labor intensive than its imports. Though responses to the paradox included, inter alia, a questioning of Leontief's statistical methods (the methods were subsequently vindicated) and his selection of 1949 as his sample period (again, results for other periods later yielded similar conclusions), there was a tendency also to question the theory Leontief sought to test.[2] For example, Vernon wrote:

> Anyone who has sought to understand the shifts in international investment over the past twenty years has chafed from time to time under an acute sense of the inadequacy of the available analytical tools. While the comparative cost concept and other basic concepts have rarely failed to provide some help, they have usually carried the analyst only a very little toward adequate understanding.
>
> . . . unless the search for better tools goes on, the usefulness of economic theory for the solution of problems in international trade and capital movements will probably decline.[3]

Several studies examined the characteristics of the pattern of U. S. trade in the post-World War II era and found that industries whose firms were most successful at exporting their products seemed characterized by relatively large firm size, high levels of research and innovation, and the use of skilled labor to a greater extent than was true for other industries.[4] In one such study Gruber, Mehta, and Vernon illustrated the importance of research and innovation (measured either by the ratio of R and D spending to total industry sales or by the ratio of scientists and engineers to total employment) in an analysis of data from 1958 and 1962 for nineteen U. S. industries (see table 1). Among their findings were:

1. The five industries that displayed the strongest research effort accounted for 72.0 percent of America's exports of manufactured products but only 39.1 percent of total sales of these products.

2. These same industries were responsible for 89.5 percent of America's total spending on R and D (including government-financed research) and 74.6 percent of company-financed expenditures.

3. Industries with the strongest research effort indicated that the majority of their R and D projects were for new products, and these same industries were dominated by large firms.

4. Capital intensity and research intensity showed no systematic correlation; economies of scale and barriers to entry stemmed from the requirements of successful product innovation and marketing, not from capital intensity.

5. The propensity for direct foreign investment was stronger in the most research-intensive industries than in the others.[5]

In another statistical analysis, using export data for 1964, Gruber and Vernon found that those industries that employed scientists and engineers in excess of 6 percent of their workforce accounted for 30 percent of the total exports of ten trading areas (i.e., either countries or regions), though they produced less than 20 percent of the total world output of manufactured goods.[6] Further, of the ten trading areas considered, exports from the United States were the most technology-intensive. United States' export shares were highest in industries with relatively few unskilled workers, low capital intensity, and high research intensity.

Mansfield, Romeo, and Wagner have also examined the effect of foreign trade on R and D.[7] In 1974 they questioned representatives of a sample of firms and about their research programs. One subgroup included twenty firms in the fabricated metals, machinery, instruments, chemical, textile, paper, and tire industries. Another subgroup consisted of ten chemical firms. For the first subgroup an average of 34 percent of an R and D project's returns was expected to come from foreign markets (either from export sales or from sales by joint ventures or controlled subsidiaries of the firms), while for the second subgroup the cor-

Table 1.   Research Effort of United States Industries, 1962

Industry	R and D as a Percentage of Total Sales	Scientists and Engineers as a Percentage of Total Employment
Transportation	10.0	3.4
Aircraft	27.2	6.9
Transportation (other)	2.8	1.0
Electrical Machinery	7.3	3.6
Instruments	7.1	3.4
Chemicals	3.9	4.1
Drugs	4.4	6.6
Other Chemicals	3.8	3.7
Machines (non-electrical)	3.2	1.4
Rubber and Plastic	1.4	0.5
Stone, Clay and Glass	1.1	*
Petroleum and Coal	0.9	1.8
Fabricated Metal	0.8	0.4
Primary Metal	0.6	0.5
Nonferrous	0.8	0.5
Ferrous	0.5	0.4
Leather	0.6	0.1
Printing and Publishing	0.6	0.2
Tobacco	0.3	0.2
Food	0.2	0.3
Textiles	0.2	0.3
Furniture and Fixtures	0.1	0.2
Lumber and Wood	0.1	*
Paper	0.1	0.3
Apparel	0.1	*
All 19 Industries	2.0	1.1
The 5 With Highest Research Effort	6.3	3.2
The 14 Other Industries	0.5	0.4

*Less than 0.5%

Note: Reprinted, by permission of the publisher, from W. Gruber, D. Mehta, and R. Vernon, "The R and D Factor in International Trade and International Investment of United States Industries," *Journal of Political Economy* 75 (1967):   23.

responding figure was 29 percent. It was also found that those firms that were the most research-intensive engaged more heavily in foreign business, and these firms expected a greater proportion of their returns to come from abroad than did other firms. Finally, all thirty firms were asked to estimate the change in their R and D expenditures (for 1974) if they had not been able to utilize any new technology abroad through their subsidiaries or if they had not been able to utilize new technology abroad by any means (subsidiary, licensing, or exporting). The results were:

Reduction in R and D Expenditures (1974)

	No Transfer Via Subsidiary	No Transfer By Any Means
1st Subsample (20 Firms)	15%	26%
2nd Subsample (10 Firms)	12%	16%

Richard Caves was among the first to analyze the foreign direct investment activities of United States MNCs within an industrial organization framework.[8] He noted that direct investments transmit equity capital, entrepreneurship, and technological or other productive knowledge in an industry-specific package. The majority of direct investments involve either horizontal expansion to produce the same product, or a similar line of product, produced initially in the MNC's home country; or, vertical integration backwards into the production of raw materials. Caves argued that for horizontal investments the transferring firm must enjoy enough of an advantage (i.e., possession of some "unique asset") to offset the information disadvantage of its alien status, and this form of transfer must be preferable to any other means of exploiting the foreign market (e.g., exporting or licensing). Often, the source of this advantage will be new or different technology or marketing expertise. A characteristic of these investments, then, is that they are for differentiated products. The firm must be able to convince potential customers that its product is superior to those of its competitors. In addition, the high fixed costs of securing information necessary to undertake foreign investments effectively exclude small firms from engaging in this activity (exporting would be a more likely method of penetrating the foreign market). Also, the varied risks of operating subsidiaries (exchange rate fluctuations, expropriation, communication costs, government instability, etc.) often lead parent firms to establish several subsidiaries in different countries. This enables MNCs to pool their risks. Caves further argued that the greater risks of operation explain why many parent firms insist on a higher expected rate of return before approving a foreign investment project than they would for a domestic investment. In summary, then, large firm size and oligopolistic industry structure, and the use of product differentiation, are characteristics of firms that transfer their production facilities abroad through subsidiaries.

There are other reasons why research tends to be carried out by relatively large firms. MNCs tend to be specialists in the production of new products; but much of their effort is geared toward product development rather than basic research or invention.[9] Product development is an expensive undertaking; Mansfield has noted that it can take five to ten years to market a new product.[10] Further, product development costs have grown over time:

Today, bringing a new drug to market requires a company to gamble as much as 10 years and $70 million, more than three times what it cost in time and money about 15 years ago. To increase the odds of success, drug makers most often look for medicines that will be useful to large numbers of people for long periods of time and then to edge out competing firms, promote the new medicines . . .[11]

The United States remains the largest mass market of high-income consumers in the world . . . The advantages imparted by the gargantuan size of the U.S. market, in fact, seemed more important in the first half of the 1970s than they had been in the 1940s. According to various fragmentary indications, the costs and risks involved with the completion of major industrial projects have been rising sharply over the decades. [For example] the cost of development of ENIACC, the computer of the early 1940s, was about $500,000, whereas IBM's 360 series was developed at a cost of about $5 billion.[12]

Of course, not all research projects will be successful. Many research-intensive firms engage in many projects at once, so that the profits from the successes will offset the losses on the failures. Mansfield surveyed 120 large companies that undertook a substantial amount of research. He concluded that

In half of these firms at least 60 percent of the research and development projects never resulted in a commercially used product or process (the smallest failure rate was 50 percent). Moreover, even when a project resulted in a product or process that was used commercially, the profitability of its use was likely to be quite unpredictable.[13]

Projects that are successful earn high rates of return; but what is sometimes thought to be "excess profit" may represent returns on past research investments which do not appear as additions to capital in the firm's books.[14]

The importance of the large size of the markets of MNCs has a subtler implication. Rosenberg has emphasized the development of a sophisticated capital goods industry as a key contributor to the long-run growth of productivity in the United States.[15] An important prerequisite for the development of this industry has been the large size of the U. S. economy. To understand this argument, consider the growth of a new firm that initially has modest sales revenue (Rosenberg followed Stigler's exposition of this point).[16] It will typically have to engage in many distinct operations (marketing, personnel training, production of inputs, etc.). However, as the market for the final product grows, the firm can begin to specialize in those operations that are most profitable. This will often afford the opportunity for other firms to provide inputs or services that the original firm had had to provide for itself. The greater the growth of the final product market, the greater the development of the auxiliary industries can be.

Rosenberg believed that the development of an efficient capital goods sector has been especially important in shifting the production functions of American industries over time.

Any cost-reduction in the capital goods sector—whether it is immediately labor-saving or capital-saving in its factor proportions bias—is capital-saving for the economy as a whole. . . . If . . . we consider the process of innovation over time, there is a high probability that labor-saving innovations are likely to be followed by capital-saving innovations . . . [a] new machine will . . . be produced inefficiently in the early stages . . . not only because there are ''bugs'' . . . but because the capital goods (machinery-producing) sector is itself not tooled or equipped for producing the machine at a low per unit cost.[17]

Baranson has provided an excellent example of the sophistication of the auxiliary industries of the United States in his exposition of the production process of a standard diesel engine, which requires more than 700 parts and components:

Over 60 percent of the dollar value of one large diesel engine manufacturer went to the procurement of components from specialized suppliers, including crankshafts, ball bearings and unfinished castings. Materials and parts are obtained from 200 different suppliers. For many parts there is a choice among several suppliers so that cost, quality and reliability can all be weighed in the exercise of choice.[18]

Both theoretical and empirical analyses suggest that the pattern of international trade and investment in the United States in the post-World War II era has been influenced by forces that have not been captured by the factor proportions theory of trade. In particular, the assumptions of given technology and perfect competition in goods and factor markets made by this theory seem particularly damaging to its predictive ability. Several attempts have been made to overcome some of the theory's shortcomings. Two of the most interesting of these are the product cycle theory of trade and the industry technology cycle theory. The following sections outline these theories and the elements they are designed to capture.

The Product Cycle Theory of Trade and Investment

Raymond Vernon developed the theory of the product cycle, which was designed to incorporate innovation, uncertainty, and scale economies into a dynamic theory of international trade and investment.[19] The Hecksher-Ohlin theorem assumes that knowledge of the same production techniques is accessible to producers in all countries. Vernon began by postulating that, while scientific knowledge may be easily and quickly diffused internationally, commercial application of this knowledge in the form of a new product requires the efforts of entrepreneurs. These efforts are not always the same across countries.

There is good reason to believe . . . that the entrepreneur's consciousness of and responsiveness to opportunity are a function of ease of communication; and further, that ease of communication is a function of geographical proximity. . . .
   The fact that the search for knowledge is an inseparable part of the decision-making process . . . [is] well-established through empirical research. One implication of that fact is that producers in any market are more likely to be aware of the possibilities of introducing new products in that market than producers located elsewhere would be.[20]

Vernon then assumed that since high unit labor costs and high per capita incomes characterize the U.S. economy, American entrepreneurs are first aware of opportunities for new products that are labor-saving or that appeal to high-income consumers. Therefore, the product cycle predicts that innovation in these areas should occur in the United States to a greater degree than in other countries.

There are three stages that new products move through in the United States, according to Vernon's theory.

New Product

In this stage an innovating firm engages in product development, i.e., the application of technology to develop a product that would likely appeal to segments of the American economy.[21] A successful innovator is likely to be the beneficiary of a high return, at least in the short run when the firm will have some monopoly power.

Vernon further argued that the location of production facilities in this stage is also likely to be in the United States. One might reason that market proximity would augur for a manufacturing location in the United States, but clearly transportation is only one of several cost variables. The extensive use of foreign production sites by MNCs illustrates the tendency for producers to respond to factor cost differences by choosing among both foreign and domestic locations.[22] Vernon's argument goes beyond consideration of manufacturing costs. A new product is likely to be "unstandardized." Specification of product design and the inputs to be used in the production process may be changed as "bugs" are worked out. Design changes may be necessary after initial marketing in order to respond to consumer desires that could not have been foreseen.

Uncertainty forces producers to place a premium on swift communication. They must have access to suppliers, consumers, and possibly other producers in order to be able to alter the dimensions of product or process. In the new product stage economies of scale will not be fully realized; as long as the product is unstandardized it cannot be mass-produced. It seems reasonable, then, that the production process will be labor-intensive; but it is not necessarily a skilled-labor-intensive stage. The premium placed on the services of scientists and engineers, and the like, is apt to be greater before the product becomes commercially successful. Vernon commented:

> In the early stages, the value-added contribution of industries engaged in producing these items probably contains an unusually high proportion of labor. . . . At this stage, the standardization of the manufacturing process has not gotten very far; that is to come later, when the volume of output is high enough and the degree of uncertainty low enough to justify investment in relatively inflexible, capital-intensive facilities . . . the production process relies relatively heavily on labor when the United States commands an export position; and the process relies more heavily on capital at a time when imports become more important.[23]

Maturing Product

As demand for the product grows, it becomes more standardized. Though there will likely be product differentiation in this stage, certain basic production methods will have become established. Economies of scale, therefore, become realizable and capital intensity increases in this stage. Other countries which have been served by American exports (initially these are likely to be nations similar to the United States in terms of labor costs and income levels) may develop into large enough markets to be served either by new domestic producers, who see an opportunity for profit, or by affiliates of U. S. firms. Less of a premium is placed upon swift communication and access to suppliers in this stage, and more regard is given to manufacturing costs at alternative locations. Consequently, an MNC may find that a plant located in a foreign country serves the foreign market (possibly including third countries) better than one located in the United States. If manufacturing costs are low enough abroad to offset transportation costs, the United States market may be served, at least partially, by imports.

Standardized Product

The third stage of the cycle occurs when the product becomes highly standardized and entrepreneurs need not incur the marketing costs associated with developing new international markets. Less developed countries may become sites for production in this stage. Such areas usually offer the advantage of ample supplies of low-cost labor, but often lack other resources: skilled labor, cheap energy supplies, adequate transportation facilities, efficient capital goods industries, and other inputs. Due to these disadvantages, many highly standardized products may never be efficiently produced in less developed countries (LDCs). Vernon holds out the possibility, however, that the prospects for locating production facilities in LDCs will likely be brighter the less producers need to rely upon local suppliers and the greater the unskilled labor intensity of production processes. Fully standardized products fulfill these requirements better than new or maturing products.

Research, Appropriability, and the Industry Technology Cycle

Multinational corporations are specialists in the development of new knowledge or technology that is embodied in products or production processes. Once new technology has been successfully developed, however, it takes on the character of a public good; that is, other firms can use the technology without incurring the research and development costs of the innovator. To the extent that new technology results from privately financed R and D, then, the prospect of rapid diffusion of new knowledge may discourage future research efforts. As Harry Johnson has written:

The dual role of knowledge as a private good in production and a public good in consumption poses an insolvable problem for a private enterprise system. If the use of knowledge is artificially restricted by the imposition and enforcement of a payment by the user to the producer, the producer is given an incentive to produce though the incentive to produce will be smaller . . . than the knowledge production is worth to society; and the level of use of the knowledge will be less than would be socially optimal. If instead a charge for the knowledge is inherently impossible to assess . . . what knowledge is created will be freely and fully used . . . but the amount of knowledge will be less than optimal, since no one will have an incentive to produce it, except as a by-product of his private satisfaction-maximizing activities . . . [24]

The realization that the returns to privately financed R and D will be likely to wane over time influences the type of research that MNCs engage in and the market structure of industries whose firms are research-intensive. Stephen Magee has developed an industry technology cycle (ITC) theory that parallels Vernon's product cycle theory and emphasizes the importance of the "public good" characteristics of new knowledge in the determination of market structure. Magee's appropriability theory (see chapter 1) of the creation of new knowledge plays a central role in the development of the industry technology cycle. The appropriability theory

suggests that multinational corporations are specialists in the production of information which is less efficient to transfer through markets than within firms; that multinational corporations produce sophisticated technologies because appropriability is higher for these technologies than for simple ones; that the large proportion of skilled labor employed by the multinationals is an outgrowth of the skilled-labor intensity of the production process for both the creation and the appropriability of the returns from information . . . and that output growth in each industry ultimately becomes information saving, i.e., the share of value added which goes to scientists and engineers in the development of new information ultimately declines. [25]

Traditionally, three types of research and development activities have been distinguished, although the distinctions among the three can sometimes be blurred. First, there is basic research, which is identified by its motive: the pursuit of new knowledge. This pursuit is not linked to any specific applications for the knowledge obtained. Basic research is often conducted in a university setting. A second type of R and D is applied research, which is directed at specific application for the knowledge that is ultimately discovered. The third type of research is product (or process) development, which involves taking research findings and converting them into a usable product or production process. It is on the third type of research that most of the efforts of large MNCs are concentrated.

By the time a project reaches the development stage, much of the uncertainty regarding its technical feasibility has been removed, but there is considerable uncertainty regarding the cost of development, time to completion, and utility of outcome. The development phase of a project is generally more expensive than the research phase. There is a long road from a preliminary sketch, showing how an invention should work, to the blueprints and specifications for the construction of the productive facilities. The tasks that are carried out depend . . . on the nature . . . of the development project. In some cases, various types of experiments must be made and prototypes must be designed and developed. Frequently, pilot plants are built and the experience with the pilot plant is studied before large-scale production is attempted.[26]

There is considerable evidence to indicate that large firm size is not necessary in order to engage successfully in basic research or invention. For example, one study has shown that almost all of the important inventions in the development of petroleum cracking processes were made by people not associated with major firms.[27] However, large size is often an advantage for firms that engage in product development, i.e., taking an invention or idea that has been proven to be technically feasible and turning it into a commercially successful product (it will be shown in a later section that there are limits to the advantages of large firm size). In the development of the ITC, Magee argued that there was a further link between industry structure and the creation of knowledge in that the presence of high industry concentration encourages research since appropriability costs are less for oligopolists than for more competitive firms. In competitive industries the greater number of potential rivals that could obtain access to new knowledge would result in low appropriability. Of course, the legal system provides ways of establishing and protecting property rights for new knowledge; but these systems serve to retard the diffusion of knowledge, not to prevent it from occurring. In addition, the legal costs of establishing and enforcing these rights may be prohibitively high for very small firms. Magee claimed that successful research leads to an increase in optimal firm size and greater concentration.

Ironically, private expenditures for preventing the loss of appropriability are public goods themselves. The first firm in an industry may obtain patents, establish legal precedents for property rights, etc.; but new entrants into the industry benefit from these efforts without having to pay the legal costs themselves. A concentrated industry structure will encourage firms to spend money on appropriability schemes since the free rider problem will be relatively minor.

Industries that begin by being research-intensive and oligopolistic, however, will eventually become both less involved in research and more competitive. Magee supported this contention with Nelson's observation that the number of patents obtained by firms in given industries follows an S-curve (see figure 1).[28] In the initial section of this curve (OA), a major innovation may have taken place. The demand for the final product may stimulate a market for component parts and servicing. The new knowledge, or technology, developed will have complementary uses for other products in the industry. Eventually, though, diminishing marginal returns to the knowledge will set in with the passage of time (AB in figure 1). Factor productivity, which would grow rapidly initially, will grow more slowly, and technological change and research activity will wane.

The appropriability theory asserts that concentrated industry structure encourages R and D and that promising inventions lead MNCs to engage in product

Figure 1

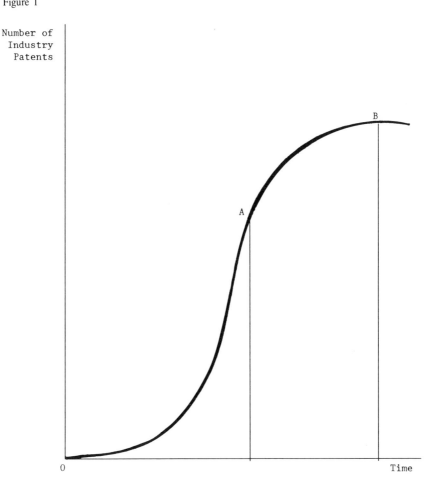

development; the returns to product development will be more appropriable if the firm expands. Therefore, Magee's reasoning led him to this hypothesis: "Young industries are concentrated and have high R and D while older ones are competitive and spend less on R and D."[29]

Magee's ITC theory may be summarized as follows:

Invention Stage

This stage precedes the commercial development of a new product. Large corporations concentrate their R and D spending on product development, and small firms historically have been the source of many inventions. Therefore, optimal firm size is relatively small. Large corporations (if they themselves are not responsible for inventions) will typically serve as buyers for information generated in this state and appropriability will be fairly high due to the legal protection given the inventor via the patent system.

Innovation Stage

As an industry ages there is an expectation that the appropriability of returns to new information will decline. In this stage, then, corporate research and marketing strategy will take this into consideration. In effect, the innovation stage encompasses the first two stages of Vernon's product cycle. Large optimum firm size and concentrated industry structure are characteristics of this stage. Firms will likely seek the creation of sophisticated products and production processes since these will be harder for other firms to imitate. Appropriability will be less in this stage than in the first.[30] Once a product is marketed, it becomes possible for another firm to "ride free" on the research investments of the innovator. A corollary to the appropriability theory is that an MNC will be expected (ceteris paribus) to prefer intrafirm transfers of new technology to foreign markets, as opposed to transfer via licensing or joint venture.

Standardization Stage

This coincides with the third stage of the product cycle. Production processes are highly standardized, appropriability is low, and optimal firm size is smaller than in the previous stage. Industry structure has become more competitive. Little new product information is generated, and firms have become less R and D intensive. Barriers to entry may, of course, still exist in an industry in this stage due to capital requirements and the like; but they will not be due to research capability requirements.

3

Tests of the Product and Industry Technology Cycles

Vernon's product cycle assumed that the pattern of technological change in a country is not random but is influenced by entrepreneurial response to factor prices and consumer tastes. In particular, one should find, according to Vernon, that the pattern of technological change in the United States reflects the desire of entrepreneurs to develop products and processes that are labor-saving and/or appeal to consumers who have relatively high incomes.

In fact, in a study of over 1,800 innovations developed between 1945 and 1974 in Japan, the United States, the United Kingdom, and other European countries, Davidson has shown that U.S. firms have a tendency to concentrate their research efforts in two main areas: new products or processes that can be identified as primarily labor-saving and those that satisfy novel demands (see table 2).[1] Out of 309 U.S. process innovations identified in Davidson's study, over 60 percent were classified as labor-saving. It is also interesting to note that the pattern of process innovation in other countries does not appear to be random. The relatively scarce supplies of land and other natural resources in Europe and Japan apparently offered incentives for producers from these areas to emphasize material-saving innovations. Similar patterns emerge from a study of the history of product innovation.

The dynamic character of the product cycle seems to explain the pattern of trade for some products. Wells provided some evidence for this.[2] Table 3 shows 1962–1963 U.S. exports of several products as a ratio of the corresponding figures for 1952–1953. Wells divided these products into three categories: necessities, discretionary items, and luxuries (although he did not define these terms). The exports of luxury products, those particularly geared towards high-income consumers, increased over 330 percent over the period covered. Wells further noted that producers of products whose costs were significantly higher that those of their substitutes (e.g., electric pencil sharpeners and knives) and those that were expensive to own and maintain compared to their substitutes (e.g., large "gas guzzler" automobiles) were able to retain an advantage in export markets due to their unique

Table 2. Process and Product Innovations Initially Introduced in the U.K., U.S., Europe and Japan, 1945–1974 Classified by Perceived Advantage

Process Innovations

Perceived Advantage	U.K. No.	U.K. %	U.K. Rank	Japan No.	Japan %	Japan Rank	Europe No.	Europe %	Europe Rank	U.S. No.	U.S. %	U.S. Rank
Capital Saving	61	23.9	3	1	28.0	1	43	24.8	2	58	18.8	4
Material Saving	122	47.8	3	12	48.1	2	95	53.7	1	58	18.8	4
Labor Saving	66	25.9	2	4	16.0	4	32	18.1	3	189	61.1	1
Multifactor Saving	6	2.4	3	2	8.0	1	7	3.9	2	4	1.3	4
Total	255	100.0		25	100.0		177	100.0		309	100.0	

Product Innovations

Perceived Advantage	U.K. No.	U.K. %	U.K. Rank	Japan No.	Japan %	Japan Rank	Europe No.	Europe %	Europe Rank	U.S. No.	U.S. %	U.S. Rank
Labor Saving	13	4.1	3	2	2.9	4	9	4.5	2	145	27.5	1
Material Saving	127	40.3	2	20	29.0	3	100	50.3	1	117	22.6	4
Novel Function/Novel Demand	50	15.9	4	12	17.4	2	33	16.6	3	106	20.5	1
Safety	49	15.5	1	7	10.1	2	11	5.5	4	50	9.7	3
Other	64	20.3	2	27	39.1	1	38	19.1	3	88	17.0	4
Multiple Advantages	12	3.8	2	1	1.4	4	8	4.0	1	14	2.8	3
Total	315	100.0		69	100.0		199	100.0		517	100.0	

Note: Reprinted, by permission of the publisher, from W. Davidson, "Patterns of Factor-Saving Innovation in the Industrialized World," European Economic Review, 8 (1976): 214–215.

Table 3. Ratio of Value of 1962–1963 Exports to Value of 1952–1953 Exports

Necessity		Discretionary		Luxury	
Refrigerators	0.47	Automobiles	0.99	Movie Cameras	4.14
Ranges	0.87	Electric Clocks	1.04	Freezers	0.74
Radios	1.42	Still Cameras	4.66	Air Conditioners	3.59
Irons	1.56	Washers	1.35	Slide Projectors	4.66
Televisions	1.04	Vacuum Cleaners	1.78	Dishwashers	8.50
		Mixers	1.25	Outboard Motors	4.18
		Record Players	1.81	Recreational Boats	4.40
Average	1.07		1.84		4.32

Note: Reprinted, by permission of the publisher, from L. T. Wells, "A Product Life Cycle for International Trade?" Journal of Marketing, 32 (1968): 4.

appeal to American consumers. In other words, few foreign producers chose to produce these types of products in the period covered but concentrated their efforts on consumer products with broader appeal in their own markets. Wells also found that the product cycle could be used to explain the development of many labor-saving products (like fork-lift trucks, computers, and construction equipment), which were first produced and exported by American producers and were later imported into the United States. However, not all products follow the pattern specified by the product cycle. This is especially true for products with a high natural resource content.[3]

Magee's industry technology cycle hypothesizes that industries move through their own cycles. To provide a theoretical foundation for the ITC, Magee applied Gaskins' dynamic limit pricing model for oligopoly industries to his analysis of large, research-oriented firms.[4] Basically, the model employs control theory to argue that an innovating firm will establish a pricing strategy that recognizes the likely entry of new competitors into its market(s). If one assumes that the firm has developed a product which has embodied within it some new knowledge or information (i.e., one cannot market the product and the innovative component separately), it will charge less than the profit-maximizing price in the short run in order to slow the entry of new firms. As new firms do eventually enter the market, the optimal strategy is for the innovator to lower its price gradually until a long-run equilibrium price (the "limit price") is reached, at which point no new firms will enter the market.[5]

Magee claimed that the ITC and the pricing model imply that "young industries are concentrated and have high R and D while older ones are competitive and spend less on R and D."[6] In support of this statement Magee found that for 1967 the simple correlation between research and development as a percentage of sales and the average industry age for 29 three-digit United States industries is $-.34$.[7] The average product age for 137 four-digit United States industries was compared to the corresponding four-firm concentration ratios. Magee reported that the "correlation between the two variables is low." He then divided the industries into two groups: those 119 with ages below and those 18 with ages above 25.5 years. He found that the difference between the means of both samples' concentration ratios is significant at the .01 level.[8]

One may question the support offered for the ITC on several grounds. With reference to the pricing model, it should be noted that the declining market share result assumed that there was a constant demand for the innovating firm's output. However, a characteristic of successful production innovation is relatively rapid market growth. As Gaskins pointed out:

> Steady growth of the product market unfortunately mitigates the decline of dominant firms and causes the long-run product price to be above the average cost of production. By-products of faster economic growth are increased concentration and higher prices in dominated markets.[9]

Gaskins' qualification does not necessarily invalidate the ITC, but it does emphasize the difficulty one would have in testing the dynamic theory. A successful innovating firm could maintain or increase its market share through rapid sales growth or continual innovation. Magee suggests that "output growth in each industry ultimately becomes information saving, i.e., the share of value added which goes to scientists and engineers in the development of new information ultimately declines."[10] It is not clear how long it would take for this process to manifest itself. Magee has little to say on this point; he stated that "the content of a stage theory is inductively derived but economically grounded in a dynamic process while the timing of the stages . . . is an empirically inspired tautology."[11]

Magee's empirical tests do not offer any insight into the dynamic character of the ITC since he used data from only one year. If one were to observe declining research intensity and concentration over time across some group of industries, this would constitute a more meaningful test of the ITC. Suppose, however, that the opposite had been found; if concentration had not fallen along with research intensity, this presumably could be used to argue that the ITC was invalid. On the other hand, another explanation is also possible: the industries were still within the innovation (second) stage of the ITC and the time period for which the data were obtained was too short to observe simultaneous declines in concentration and research intensity.

Indeed, even a finding of reduced concentration over time need not imply diminished appropriability of research. The most concentrated industries may simply be "regressing towards the mean." That is, the high initial concentration may be due to transitory factors that will be reversed later. Further, it is not clear what the time period for such a study would have to be. Consistent market share data for many four-digit U.S. industries are available only from 1947. Due to changes in industry coverage and definition, meaningful studies of concentration changes over a broad range of industries may be possible only over a ten to twenty-five year period.

One may also take issue with Magee's use of the variable measuring industry age. He measures industry age by subtracting the average "first-trade-date" of products of each industry from 1967. This variable was first developed by Gary Hufbauer.[12] Hufbauer examined various editions (from 1909 to 1965) of the Census Bureau's export classification list, or Schedule B. The 1965 edition listed export commodities at the seven-digit SITC level (about 1,000 items were included in the classification), and he determined the arrival of these products into the international export market by noting, in previous years' Schedule B listings, the year that each first appeared. By taking an unweighted average of these years, he constructed industry average ages at the three-digit level. The range of first trade dates was found to be 1927.7 to 1954.6.

Hufbauer warned, however, that "the first trade dates very inadequately reflect the commodity characteristics they purport to measure."[13] Some dates seemed to contradict a priori expectations (e.g., cotton fabrics had a first trade date of 1952.6 while electrical apparatus for medical purposes had a date of 1944.7). Certain commodity groups formed by combinations of other groups and some categories with more than one commodity could not be traced to an initial trade date. There is also a bias towards creating new product categories in instances where total export value figures were relatively large.

Another of Magee's propositions is that a successful innovation leads to an increase in optimal firm size, and as a consequence, greater industry concentration. There has been little empirical evidence, at the level of the firm or industry, on the extent to which technological change is scale-increasing. Using a computer simulation model, Nelson and Winter have found that a rapid rate of technological change appears to be associated with a relatively high level of industry concentration, but they were careful to point out the tentative nature of their conclusions.[14] One important empirical study of this hypothesis was conducted by Mansfield, who obtained data on the proportion of major innovations that were scale-increasing (i.e., resulted in increases in minimum efficient scale of plant) for nine chemical firms, twelve petroleum firms, and four steel firms.[15] A random sample of thirty-five process innovations in these industries was selected, and representatives of the firms surveyed were able to determine the effects of the innovations on plant size. The results of the survey are shown in table 4.

For the period covered (years since 1920), there was a clear tendency for process innovations to be scale-increasing. In the steel industry the tendency was less pronounced, but few of the innovations were scale-decreasing. Other data were obtained for thirty-one product innovations of the surveyed firms and how these affected the four-firm concentration ratios of their respective industries. These results, also shown in table 4, are especially interesting since the majority of firms' R and D efforts is for product, rather than process, development. The definition of market for the determination of the effect on concentration was aided by input from the surveyed firms. Perhaps the most interesting result obtained was for drug firms. As Mansfield observed:

> In the petroleum and steel industries, the concentration-increasing product innovations greatly outnumbered the concentration-decreasing product innovations. But in the chemical industry there were almost as many concentration-decreasing innovations as concentration-increasing innovations; and in the drug industry, the concentration-decreasing innovations outnumbered the concentration-increasing innovations. . . . Moreover, sampling errors are very unlikely to have been responsible for concentration-decreasing innovations being a substantial percentage of the total in the drug and chemical industries combined. If concentration-decreasing innovations were much fewer than concentration-increasing innovations in these industries combined, the probability that my results would have occurred is less than 0.04.[16]

As it turns out, over one-half of the drug product innovations were by firms entering new product markets or by firms that were not among the four largest firms in the industry. Mansfield tested whether the rate of productivity advance

Table 4. Percentage Distribution of Major New Processes by Effect on Minimum Efficient Scale of Plant and of Major New Products by Effect on Four-Firm Concentration Ratio

Effect of Process or Product	Chemicals (1929-76)	Drugs (1947-78)	Petroleum (1919-76)	Steel (1919-60)
Percentage Distribution of Major New Processes, by Effect on Minimum Efficient Scale of Plant				
Increase	92	---	75	43
No Effect	8	---	25	43
Decrease	0	---	0	14
Total	100		100	100
Percentage Distribution of Major New Products, by Effect on Four-firm Concentration Ratio				
Increase	43	17	60	43
No Effect	29	8	40	57
Decrease	29	75	0	0
Total	100[a]	100	100	100

[a]Because of rounding errors, figures do not sum to total.

Note: Reprinted, by permission of the publisher, from E. Mansfield, "Technological Change and Market Structure," American Economic Review (p), 73 (1983): 206.

was related to the percent of industry product (or process) innovations that were scale-increasing for various ten-to-fifteen-year time periods. For the industries in the survey, there was no significant relationship found when productivity growth was regressed on the percentage of scale-increasing product or process innovations. Another regression that used R and D expenditures as a ratio of industry sales as a dependent variable did not produce a statistically significant relationship either. Finally, Mansfield examined the correlation between industry productivity growth (and alternatively, R and D expenditures divided by value-added) and the change in the average four-firm concentration ratio of all two-digit manufacturing industries (the time periods chosen for the correlations were not reported). The coefficient of correlation between productivity growth and the change in concentration was found to be generally negative (that is, increases in concentration were associated with lower rates of productivity growth than decreases in concentration). The coefficient of correlation between R and D divided by value-added and change in concentration was found to be negative, and not statistically significant.[17]

Further evidence concerning the relationships between R and D and industry characteristics was obtained for seventy-nine four-digit SIC (Standard Industrial Classification) industries. Disaggregated research expenditure data are difficult to obtain. For example, most National Science Foundation data for R and D spending by U. S. industries are available at only a two-digit SIC level. Still another difficulty is raised by the interpretation of industrial R and D. Research spending by a firm in one industry may be used to develop a product or process that is used by a firm in some other industry. Recently, a new set of disaggregated research data has become available. The data were derived from a 1974 Line of Business survey conducted by the Federal Trade Commission. The survey obtained research expenditures of 443 large U.S. corporations. The research data have been linked to patents for 15,112 inventions. The patents were examined to ascertain the industry of origin and the industries that were likely to use the patents. The data are especially interesting because a matrix was devised to enable the effect of research to be traced to various industries. The technology matrix was developed under the direction F. M. Scherer:

> The linked R & D, inflated by origin industry sampling ratios, was then distributed through a "technology flows" matrix from industries of use (including personal consumption). R & D dollars for inventions of widespread use were allocated in proportion to sales of the origin industry to using industries, as ascertained from 1972 U.S. input-output tables (modified inter alia to integrate current and capital accounts transactions). Row sums for the technology flows matrix measured R & D by industry of origin, column sums R & D by industry of use, and diagonal elements correspond to pure process R & D.[18]

Although Scherer's research data are somewhat crude, they represent an important source of new information.[19] They were used to obtain R and D expenditures as a ratio of industry output (RDO) and R and D "used" as a ratio of industry output (RDU) for each of seventy-nine industries. Table 5 presents a breakdown of these industries into their respective two-digit classifications. In order to test some of the hypotheses of the ITC, correlations were computed between the two measures of research intensity and various market structure variables.[20] Table 6 presents these correlations for all of the industries in the sample and two subgroups of industries. Thirty-seven of the industries were in the SIC 35 or 36 industry groups. These two industry groups, machinery and electric and electronic equipment, produce products that are typically purchased by firms in other industries. In addition, product (rather than process) innovation is especially high in these two industries. For these reasons separate correlations were computed for SIC 35 and 36 industries and for all other industries. Table 7 presents correlations for still two other industry subgroups: the most research-intensive industries (SIC 28, 35, 36, 37, and 38; this grouping is based on the breakdown shown in table 1) and all other industries.

Research data were only available for 1974. However, there is a high correlation among the National Science Foundation's industry R and D for various years (e.g., the correlation between R and D/sales ratios for 1963 and 1973 is over 0.95).[21] Assuming that the research data here share this correlation, some tentative conclusions may be drawn from the results presented in tables 6 and 7. There appears to be no positive correlation between research intensity and industry concentration, as measured by 1977 four-firm concentration ratios. Although the industry coverage is not comprehensive, there is no support shown for Magee's claim that research-intensive industries will be more concentrated than other industries. In

Table 5. Breakdown of 79 Four-Digit SIC Industries by
Two-Digit Classification

	Two-digit SIC Industry	Number of Four-digit Industries in Sample
20	Food and Kindred Products	12
26	Paper and Allied Products	1
28	Chemicals and Allied Products	4
30	Rubber and Miscellaneous Plastics Products	1
32	Stone, Clay and Glass Products	5
33	Primary Metal Industries	4
34	Fabricated Metal Products	6
35	Machinery, except Electrical	25
36	Electric and Electronic Equipment	12
37	Transportation	3
38	Instruments and Related Products	4
39	Miscellaneous Manufacturing Industries	2
	Total	79

Table 6. Correlation Coefficients for Selected Variables (79 Four-Digit SIC Industries)

All Industries	CR77	CR73	Z63	Z67	G63	G67	PROD63	PROD67
Research Variable:								
RDU	-.09	-.11	.05	-.06	.38***	.25***	.28***	.18*
Industries	79	77	77	79	79	79	79	79
RDO	-.03	-.12	.16	-.19	.41***	.30***	.24**	.20**
Industries	79	77	77	79	79	79	79	79
Without SIC 35 & 36								
Research Variable:								
RDU	-.26**	-.31**	.14	.10	.33**	.25**	.23*	.20*
Industries	42	42	42	42	42	42	42	42
RDO	-.21*	-.30**	.24*	.19	.19	.04	.09	.04
Industries	42	42	42	42	42	42	42	42
SIC 35 & 36 Only								
Research Variable:								
RDU	.06	.07	-.01	-.14	.47***	.27*	.33**	.17
Industries	37	35	35	37	37	37	37	37
RDO	.04	.07	.10	-.27	.58***	.48***	.34**	.28**
Industries	37	35	35	37	37	37	37	37

*Statistically significant at the .10 level
**Statistically significant at the .05 level
***Statistically significant at the .01 level.

Note: RDU and RDO are ratios of research spending with respect to constant dollar (1972) industry output. RDU refers to research embodied in purchases of inputs by one industry from all others. RDO refers to research spending by industry of origin. CR77 and CR63 are four-firm digit concentration ratios, while Z63 and Z67 refer to changes in concentration ratios (CR77 minus CR63 and CR77 minus CR67, respectively). G63 and G67 measure the annual average growth of constant dollar industry output between 1963 and 1967, and between 1967 and 1977, respectively. PROD63 and PROD67 are measures of the average annual change in industry output (in 1972 dollars) per-worker-hour.

Table 7. Correlation Coefficients and Mean Values for Industry Variables (79 Four-Digit SIC Industries)

		CR77	CR63	Z63	Z67	G63	G67	PROD63	PROD67
Research-Intensive Industries[a]									
Correlations with:									
RDU		.02	-.01	.06	- .08	.25**	.12	.25**	.12
	Industries	48	46	46	46	48	48	48	48
RDO		.01	.08	.22*	.21*	.36**	.28**	.23*	.20*
	Industries	48	46	46	48	48	48	48	48
All Other Industries									
Correlations with:									
RDU		-.29*	-.30**	.04	.03	.79***	.68***	.39**	.32**
	Industries	31	31	31	31	31	31	31	31
RDO		-.30	-.31**	.05	.01	.67***	.52***	.05	.01
	Industries	31	31	31	31	31	31	31	31
Research-Intensive Industries[a]									
Mean Values		44.6	46.0	-1.7	-1.9	.041	.025	.026	.026
All Other Industries									
Mean Values		44.5	45.7	-1.3	-1.1	.028	.021	.022	.021

[a]These are industries from SIC numbers 28, 35, 36, 37, and 38.

* Statistically significant at the .10 level.

** Statistically significant at the .05 level.

***Statistically significant at the .01 level.

Note: Variable definitions are given in Table 6.

fact, the correlations indicated that there is a statistically significant negative correlation between research intensity and concentration for non-research-intensive industries (table 7). As an additional test of the concentration-research relationship, correlations were also computed using 1963 concentration ratios;[22] results were similar in each case to those obtained with the 1977 ratios.

Magee further assumed that optimal firm size and increased concentration would result from innovation. However, the change in concentration (from 1963 to 1977 and from 1967 to 1977) shows no consistent relationship with either RDO or RDU. Surely, this is due in part to the influence of other factors that affect concentration. Although research and innovation undoubtedly do cause increases in concentration in certain circumstances, as Mansfield's results suggest, the nature of the technology developed and its source (which could be either a small or large firm) may cause increased or decreased concentration.

There is support for Magee's hypothesis that market and productivity growth are positively related to research intensity. Statistically significant relationships were found for the seventy-nine-industry sample and the subsamples. However, there were some differences between the subsamples in terms of the influence of RDO and RDU. For the SIC 35 and 36 subsample and the research-intensive industries, RDO has a stronger correlation with productivity growth than it has for other industries. This result may reflect the greater reliance of the latter group of industries on innovation "imported" from other firms and the emphasis on research for product innovations embodied in new products "exported" by research-intensive firms. Finally, table 7 shows that average concentration ratios and their changes between 1963 and 1977 are very similar for the research-intensive and other industries.

Although the results shown in tables 6 and 7 should be interpreted with caution, they suggest that the effects of R and D and the link between R and D and other market structure variables are subtle and complex. It is difficult to make broad generalizations since many factors influence market concentration and productivity advance and measures of these variables are often crude. The effects of RDO and RDU are especially interesting since these effects seem to vary by industry.

Transfer of Technology to Foreign Markets

Multinational firms have several options when they seek to sell their products in foreign markets. They may export to these markets, establish subsidiaries in the foreign markets (these may be wholly-owned, majority-owned, or minority-owned joint ventures), or license the rights to produce their products to an independent firm. Some economists have tried to explain why a firm might favor one type of vehicle over another. In the product cycle Vernon postulates that new products would be exported to foreign markets but that eventually (in the maturing product stage) subsidiaries would be established that would substitute for at least part of the export trade. Some analysts viewed the process of market penetration as one of obtaining ever-increasing control over foreign operations.[23] First, the theory goes, a firm will export in order to familiarize itself with the market. Then it may license its product before ultimately acquiring equity control (either by acquiring an existing firm or setting up a new one).

However, empirical studies have cast doubt on whether the above explanations correctly describe MNC behavior. Stopford and Wells, in a survey of 187 firms, found that for the first five years of each firm's foreign market experiences, there was a preference for controlled subsidiary as a transfer medium.[24] They also found that the choice of transfer vehicle was strongly related to certain product and/or industry characteristics. The desire for subsidiary transfer was strongest, ceteris paribus, for: (a) firms that were heavily engaged in generating new products; (b) firms that relied heavily on marketing and advertising; (c) firms that were relatively large and could therefore afford to allocate managerial and other resources outside the home base; and (d) firms that engaged in limited product diversification.

Behrman and Schmidt reported the results of a survey of 162 companies known to have had an interest in licensing and 220 companies chosen from the 1,000 largest United States companies with at least one foreign subsidiary.[25] In all, responses were obtained from 207 firms, with the number of responses varying by question (data were for 1954). Fifty-seven firms responded to the question: "Was licensing a precursor to investment abroad?" Replies were distributed according to whether the firms used licensing prior to investment in all, a majority, a minority, or none of the cases of foreign operation. The results were: all—14, majority—13, minority—10, and none—20. Another question was: "Have you licensed the manufacture of an item abroad without having already exported it to that market?" The results were: all—2, majority—17, minority—19, and none—12. Still another asked: "Have you licensed the manufacture of an item abroad and later manufactured it yourself in that country?" The results were: all—0, majority—0, minority—4, and none—47. The authors concluded:

> The licensor has more frequently than not licensed the manufacture of the product abroad without having tested the market by exports; he practically never manufactured the item himself abroad in a territory after a license was granted therein . . . [26]

Another licensing survey was conducted by the Conference Board for the 1961 to 1967 period.[27] The sample consisted of 660 firms. Over 1,700 new licensing agreements were entered into by the respondents to the survey over the sample period (about 300 firms replied to the questionnaires). The survey found that the dividing lines among licensing, exporting, and direct investment had become increasingly blurred, with all three being combined at times in agreements with affiliate firms. More than one-half of the licensing agreements were accounted for by companies with annual sales revenues of less than $50 million. Company officials were asked to appraise their licensing experience. Seventy-five percent expressed satisfaction; about one-half stated that they were moving away from licensing and towards controlling subsidiaries, while 42 percent were firmly set against reducing their licensing activity in favor of a greater number of subsidiary transfers. The Conference Board concluded that the evidence seemed to show a strong preference for equity control even among companies that were not dissatisfied with their licensing experience.

Mansfield, Romeo, and Wagner estimated the preference for transfer vehicle for twenty-three firms.[28] Table 8 shows the percentage of all R and D projects where the principal mode of transfer was of each type (note that "joint venture" in the table refers to minority-owned subsidiary) for the first five years after commercialization of the new technology. Transfer via majority-owned subsidiary was overwhelmingly favored, especially for the most profitable projects:

> The great preponderance of cases where foreign subsidiaries are regarded as the principle channel . . . is noteworthy, because, according to the traditional view, the first channel of international technology transfer often is exports . . . our results may reflect an increased tendency for new technology to be transferred directly to overseas subsidiaries or a tendency for it to be transferred more quickly to them (in part because more such subsidiaries already exist). . . .
>
> Table [8] indicates that firms are more likely to license innovations that are only marginally profitable . . . they are more likely to transfer very profitable innovations via subsidiaries . . . this may reflect . . . reluctance to provide foreign producers with information and legal rights . . . [29]

Some additional data were obtained for six of the seven chemical firms surveyed to estimate the preferred transfer vehicle in the second five years after commercialization. The authors found the corresponding percentages to be: (a) foreign subsidiaries—60 percent; (b) exports—15 percent; (c) licensing—18 percent; (d) joint ventures—6 percent (compare these with the second row of the table). These results suggest that the product cycle theory's prediction of initial foreign market penetration by exports is incorrect; or at least, it is less valid than it was in years past. "Thus, the 'export stage' of the product cycle has often been truncated and sometimes eliminated."[30] There is also evidence that U. S. MNCs are transferring technology to some of their subsidiaries more quickly in recent years than in the past.

> Based on a carefully selected sample of sixty-five technologies, the mean age of the technologies transferred by U.S.-based firms to overseas subsidiaries in developed countries during 1960–78 was about six years. . . . Between 1960–68 and 1969–78, there seemed to be a significant increase in the proportion of relatively new technology transferred to subsidiaries in developed countries. But for technologies transferred to subsidiaries in developing countries or for those transferred through channels other than subsidiaries, there appeared to be no such tendency, at least in this sample.[31]

Table 8. Percentage Distribution of R and D Projects, by Anticipated Channel of International Technology Transfer, First Five Years after Commercialization, 23 Firms, 1974[1]

Category	Majority-Owned Subsidiary	Channel of Technology Transfer			Total[2]
		Exports	Licensing	Joint Venture	
All R and D Projects:					
16 Industrial Firms	85	9	5	0	100
7 Major Chemical Firms	62	21	12	5	100
Projects Aimed At[3]:					
Entirely New Product	72	4	24	0	100
Product Improvement	69	9	23	0	100
Entirely New Process	17	83	0	0	100
Process Improvement	45	53	2	1	100
Projects Whose Estimated Rates of Return Are[4]:					
Less Than 20%	36	19	38	7	100
20% to 39%	46	29	19	5	100
40% or More	100	0	0	0	100

[1]Only projects for which foreign returns are of some importance are included (more than 10 percent of total returns for the 16 industrial firms and over 25 percent for the 7 chemical firms).

[2]Percentages may not add to 100 because of rounding

[3]Only 6 chemical firms could be included.

[4]Only 4 chemical firms could be included.

Note: Reprinted, by permission of the publisher, from E. Mansfield, A. Romeo, and S. Wagner, "Foreign Trade and U.S. Research and Development," Review of Economics and Statistics 61 (1974): 55.

An unmistakable trend in the post-World War II period has been for the number of subsidiaries in countries to increase. Table 9 shows the number of such subsidiaries in Germany, France, and the United Kingdom for 1950 and 1970. Some economists have claimed that this represents a series of "defensive investments" by MNCs. The hypothesis that has frequently been advanced is that, after one firm establishes a subsidiary, its domestic competitors fear a loss of (global) market share. Vernon at one time questioned the wisdom of firms that played "follow the leader":

> Any hypothesis based on the assumption that the United States entrepreneurs will react rationally when offered the possibility of a low-cost location abroad is, of course, somewhat suspect. The decision-making sequence . . . is not a model of the rational process.[32]

With time, though, Vernon's views were altered:

> That tendency . . . was at first belittled as a slightly irrational bandwagon effect. . . . Later on . . . the . . . pattern came to be recognized as a rational form of risk-minimizing behavior . . . [33]

Magee views the process of direct investment as explicable within the framework of the ITC and the appropriability theory; i.e., the entry of new subsidiaries into foreign markets may be the result of the increased competition that takes place as an industry ages. Rents to the innovator(s) may diminish as appropriability diminishes over time. It could be that the latecomers are free riding on the investments in knowledge of their rivals. Therefore, an initial marketing success by one firm in a country may blaze a trail for others. Further, it is Magee's contention that licensing should become a more popular transfer medium as an industry moves through the innovation stage of the ITC. The preference for subsidiary transfer is strong while the technology transferred is relatively new (notice that this is consistent with the findings of Mansfield, Romeo, and Wagner) in order to maximize appropriability. As the technology ages, however, the desire for control (and, therefore, transfer via subsidiary) should decline as appropriability diminishes. Another reason for licensing to be rare for new technology is that it is difficult for a buyer to determine its market value without some previous experience to go by. The larger the number of previous transfers, the easier it is to assess a technology's market value.[34]

David Teece has presented other evidence that supports Magee's hypothesis.[35] He interviewed businessmen employed by MNCs engaged in twenty-six different international technology transfer projects. All projects were cases of design transfer (i.e., the transfer of the capacity to manufacture a product in the host country). He sought to measure the extent and variation in the costs of these transfers. Transfer costs were defined to include: (a) costs of pre-engineering, technological exchanges; (b) engineering costs associated with transferring process design; (c) costs of R

Table 9. Number of Multinational Enterprises in Selected Product Lines

Product Line	Germany 1950	Germany 1970	France 1950	France 1970	U.K. 1950	U.K. 1970
Yarn and Thread Mills	4	24	3	22	4	19
Pulp Mills	2	13	2	12	2	13
Miscellaneous Converted Paper Products	3	32	3	31	4	35
Blast Furnaces and Basic Steel Products	2	36	2	33	6	33
Iron and Steel Foundries	1	28	1	28	1	25
Primary Nonferrous Metals	5	26	6	24	9	28
Miscellaneous Primary Metal Products	3	32	4	29	3	35
Metal Cans and Shipping Containers	1	17	1	15	4	20
Fabricated Structural Metal Products	2	35	2	28	5	37
Miscellaneous Fabricated Metal Products	5	62	8	55	10	66
Beverages	2	24	3	29	10	31
Cigarettes	1	3	0	3	3	4
Drugs	6	38	10	39	23	43
Soap, Cleaners and Toilet Goods	10	40	10	43	22	48

Note: Reprinted, by permission of the publisher, from R. Vernon, Storm Over the Multinationals (Cambridge: Harvard University Press, 1977): 76.

and D (salaries and expenses incurred during all phases of the transfer) associated with developing the process; (d) pre-startup training and excess manufacturing costs (i.e., learning and debugging costs sustained during the startup phase before the plants met design performance specifications).

The highlights of Teece's findings are:

1.   Transfer costs ranged from 2 percent to 59 percent of total project costs. The average figure was 19 percent.

2.   The first subsample included firms in the machinery industry. The second subsample included firms in the petroleum refining and chemicals industries. Transfer costs were higher, on average, in the first subsample. Large cost reductions occurred in the first subsample as the years of manufacturing experience of the recipient increased and as the age of the technology increased. This was attributed to the fact that learning economies are relatively important in the machinery industry.

3. In the petroleum and chemicals subsample of firms, transfer costs fell significantly as the number of previous startups of a similar project increased.

4. There was little evidence to indicate that a transferee had to be either very large or very R and D intensive to successfully absorb manufacturing know-how.

5. Officials of the surveyed firms were asked to estimate how transfer costs would vary under certain conditions. The results indicated that these costs would be lowest (ceteris paribus) when the transferee was a majority-owned subsidiary, higher for joint ventures, higher still for licensing to a private firm, and highest if the transfer were to a government enterprise. The increase was particularly sharp for the machinery subsample. Since transfers were found to be declining cost processes, the differences among the costs for these transfer media would become less over time.

From the standpoint of transfer costs, therefore, MNCs seem more likely to choose transfer via subsidiary when their projects are new. Over time this preference seems to decrease as costs fall; licensing then becomes more popular.

Firm Size, Industry Concentration, and Research Intensity: Empirical Estimates

The link that Magee made between market structure and research and innovation has been examined often in the past. Perhaps no one is more closely associated with the notion that some degree of oligopoly is necessary for technological innovation than Joseph Schumpeter:

> What we have got to accept is that [the large-scale establishment] has come to be the most powerful engine of [economic] progress. . . . In this respect, perfect competition is not only impossible but inferior, and has no title to being set up as a model of ideal efficiency.[36]

Few would dispute the contention that very competitive firms can ill afford large amounts of research and development and the attendant risks involved with extensive product development. However, one travels a long road in moving from pure competition to monopoly. It is, indeed, valid to argue that large firms' size and/or high market concentration could at some point inhibit innovation since: (a) a dominant firm feeling little potential competitive pressure from (present or prospective) rivals may not be spurred to innovate vigorously; and (b) the organizational structure of a large firm may not be conducive to bold decision-making. The diversification effort of Exxon Corporation in the early 1980s provides a textbook example of the difficulties that very large firms may have in making decisions. After sixteen years Exxon abandoned some of its mining operations that had produced large losses. A former manager at Exxon attributed part of the company's problems to an unwieldly organizational structure that can sometimes stifle initiative. "Authority is usually vested in numerous . . . committees rather than individuals who can and want to be held accountable."[37] Though still very successful with its petroleum operations, Exxon has stubbed its toes on new ventures. Critics blame a tendency to "over-study" major proposals; by the time a decision has to be made, many dollars and much time may have been spent. As an example of this sluggishness, another former Exxon employee cited the study of a proposal to sell a uranium tailings pond. For over six months Exxon officials and outside consultants considered the issue. "We ran one computer run after another. . . . We spent so much time studying it, it cost us more than we could have ever gotten out of it."[38]

In commenting on the frustration that can result from working for a large firm, Scherer noted that

> During the two decades following World War II, thousands of research-based new enterprises were founded by frustrated fugitives of such U.S. giants as Sperry-Rand, IBM, Western Electric, Hughes Aircraft, Raytheon, and many others.[39]

More formal studies of the link between innovation and market structure also support a less extreme form of the Schumpeterian hypothesis. For example, Worley examined the numbers of research and development (laboratory) personnel employed by 198 firms in 1955.[40] All but three of these firms had at least 5,000 (total) employees. The mean, median, and range of research personnel per 1,000 employees for these firms were computed and broken into eight industry groups (Worley's figures are shown in table 10). The data showed that firms near the middle of the industry distribution hired more research personnel than firms at either end; and in four of the eight industries, the firm employing the relatively greatest number of research personnel was smaller (using total employment as a measure of firm size) than the firm employing the smallest number of employees.

Worley then ran a regression based on the equation:

$$Y = AX^b$$

where:

Y = the number of persons employed in research development
X = total firm employment

Logs were taken of the equation and separate regressions were run for each of the industry groups:

$$\log Y = \log A + b \log X$$

Table 10. Research and Development Personnel per One Thousand
Employees among Large Firms in Eight Industry Groups (1955)

Industry Group	R and D Personnel Per 1000 Employees			
	No. of Firms	Mean	Median	Range
Food & Kindred Products	25	11.6	8.1	0.4 - 43.5
Chemicals & Allied Products	29	50.3	44.7	9.0 - 109.4
Petroleum & Petroleum Products	24	27.3	27.6	4.7 - 58.5
Stone, Clay & Glass Products	16	14.6	9.6	2.7 - 39.6
Primary Metals	24	5.8	3.6	1.2 - 23.6
Machinery (except electrical)	26	22.1	10.4	3.0 - 95.0
Electrical Machinery	25	48.8	36.0	3.3 - 201.1
Transportation Equipment	29	25.5	21.4	1.4 - 91.8
Total	198			

Note: Reprinted, by permission of the publisher, from J. Worley, "Industrial Research and the New Competition," Journal of Political Economy 59 (1961): 184.

The coefficient b, then, measured the elasticity of research personnel with respect to firm size. The results of these regressions are shown in table 11. Worley tested (using a one-tail t test) the hypothesis that b was greater than unity. If b were to exceed unity, this obviously would indicate ever-greater research intensity with increased firm size. For the petroleum and electrical machinery industries b was significant at the .05 and .10 levels of probability, respectively. For the other six industries, b was not significantly different from one.

Comanor also studied this issue with data from the 1955 to 1960 time period. He grouped 387 firms into twenty-one three-digit industries and then computed firm size elasticities, whose interpretation is similar to the interpretation of Worley's elasticities. Firm size was measured by average employment between 1955 and 1960, and the level of research was represented by two variables: (a) the average numbers of all research personnel in 1955 and 1960 and (b) a similar average for professional research personnel (see table 12). Comanor found that

> The elasticities estimated for professional research personnel exceed unity in only six cases out of twenty-one, and these differences are never statistically significant . . . the estimated coefficients are significantly less than one in seven cases out of twenty-one.[41]

Similar results were reported for the other elasticity when total research person-

Table 11. Worley's Regression Results: Measurement of the Elasticity of Research Personnel with Respect to Firm Size

Industry Groups	No. of Firms	b	t-Statistic
Food & Kindred Products	25	0.638	-1.316
Chemicals & Allied Products	29	1.071	+0.480
Petroleum & Petroleum Products	24	1.229	+2.009
Stone, Clay & Glass Products	16	1.317	+1.210
Primary Metals	24	0.885	-0.590
Machinery (except electrical)	26	1.226	+0.801
Electrical Machinery	25	1.285	+1.418
Transportation Equipment	29	1.011	+0.060
Total	198		

Note: Reprinted, by permission of the publisher, from J. Worley, "Industrial Research and the New Competition," Journal of Political Economy 59 (1961): 185.

nel was used as a research measure. Elasticities for this group exceeded unity in ten cases, with only one of them being significantly greater than one. Again, seven industries had coefficients significantly less than one. Both Worley and Comanor, then, find support for the notion that in some industries smaller firms undertake research in proportions that exceed their relative market sizes.

Of course, one must be careful to qualify what is meant by "small"; but a consensus view seems to be that research has a "threshold effect" in many U.S. industries. In a study of the petroleum, drug, glass and steel industries (data were taken from the 1945–1959 period) Mansfield found that there was "no evidence that the largest firms in these industries spend more . . . on R and D, relative to sales, than somewhat smaller firms."[42] Mansfield's work is of interest since instead of examining only measures of research input (e.g., R and D spending or employment), he uses data for the productivity of research in these industries. Similar conclusions were obtained by Scherer, who used as a measure of research output the number of patents obtained by 352 of the Fortune 500 firms in 1959.[43] As examination of both 1955 sales and employment showed that the largest firms accounted for a smaller share of both research inputs and outputs than their shares of the total sales of all 352 firms (see table 13).

In summaries of the above-mentioned studies, and others, Markham and Scherer note that in spite of differences in approach, variables, and time periods

Table 12. Research—Firm Size Elasticities[a]
(Firm Size Measured by Number of Employees)

Industry	No. of Firms	Elasticity for Professional Research Personnel	Elasticity for Total Research Personnel
Foods	36	1.07 (0.19)	1.12 (0.20)
Cigarettes	5	0.85 (0.44)	1.06 (0.60)
Textiles	13	0.23 (0.17)	0.41 (0.14)
Paper & Allied Products	26	0.59 (0.09)	0.70 (0.09)
Industrial Chemicals	23	0.83 (0.12)	0.92 (0.11)
Drugs	19	0.53 (0.11)	0.60 (0.13)
Soaps & Cosmetics	14	0.70 (0.16)	0.75 (0.18)
Petroleum	22	1.11 (0.10)	1.23 (0.10)
Tires & Tubes	8	1.05 (0.06)	1.08 (0.08)
Stone, Clay & Glass	25	0.68 (0.11)	0.80 (0.12)
Steel	24	0.67 (0.14)	0.67 (0.15)
Non-Ferrous Metals	25	0.37 (0.08)	0.39 (0.08)
Farm & Construction Machinery	14	0.95 (0.16)	1.05 (0.18)
Industrial Machinery	25	0.78 (0.13)	0.86 (0.14)
Office Machinery	9	0.80 (0.26)	0.95 (0.25)
Electrical Equipment	20	1.17 (0.16)	1.24 (0.15)
Household Appliances	12	0.95 (0.12)	1.07 (0.14)
Communication Equipment	15	0.91 (0.16)	1.01 (0.17)
Motor Vehicles	12	1.02 (0.12)	1.06 (0.12)
Aircraft	21	1.07 (0.11)	1.00 (0.13)
Instruments	19	0.53 (0.12)	0.61 (0.13)

[a]Figures in parentheses are standard errors of the coefficients.

Note: Reprinted, by permission of the publisher, from W. Comanor, "Market Structure, Product Differentiation, and Industrial Research," Quarterly Journal of Economics, 81 (1967): 642-643.

used to examine research and market structure, there is general agreement that the research threshold for firms may be represented by: (a) less than $200 million in yearly sales at 1955 price levels or (b) roughly 5,000 total employees.[44] Roughly speaking, the size of the last of the Fortune 500 firms in any year establishes the size above which one would not expect ever-greater returns to research intensity.

However, the relationship between firm size and concentration and research varies by industry. Comanor reasoned that product differentiation is one motivation for innovation (especially for new products) and that the effect of research on concentration may vary by industry depending on the extent of interindustry

Table 13. Concentration of Sales, Patents, and R and D Employment
in a Sample of 352 Large Corporations

Number of Firms, Ranked by 1955 Sales	Percentage of Total for All 352 Firms		
	1955 Sales	1955 R & D Employment	1959 Patents
First 4	19.9	9.7	10.4
First 8	27.5	16.4	16.8
First 12	32.8	25.9	24.9
First 20	41.5	36.7	32.9
First 30	49.0	44.7	42.9
First 40	55.0	50.4	45.0
First 50	59.9	57.8	50.8
First 100	75.9	71.9	71.0
First 200	90.8	90.0	89.4
First 300	97.7	97.8	97.4
All 352	100.0	100.0	100.0

Note: Reprinted, by permission of the publisher, from F. M. Scherer, Industrial
Market Structure and Economic Performance (Chicago: Rand McNally, 1970):
360.

product differentiation.[45] In fact, he found some tendency for high concentration ratios to be associated with high research in industries that are characterized by low product differentiation. In support of his view, Mansfield found that the composition of R and D efforts, in addition to their size, also varies by firm and industry. He obtained data from 108 firms for 1977 (all firms surveyed had spent over $10 million on R and D in 1976).[46] The research data were broken into several categories, and regressions were run in order to determine to what extent increases in firm size were associated with increases in basic R and D, relatively long-term R and D (that is, for projects lasting at least five years), and R and D for risky projects (those with no more than an estimated 50 percent chance of technical and commercial success). There was some tendency for increases in firm size to lead to greater than proportional increases in spending for basic research but little evidence that increases in firm size were associated with greater than proportional increases in any of the other categories of research spending. Substantial interfirm and interindustry variation was found for these relationships. Correlation coefficients showed little evidence of a relationship between four-firm four-digit SIC industry concentration ratios and any of the four categories of research spending.

4

Market Structure, Profitability, and Efficiency

Many studies have examined the relationship between industrial concentration and profits among U.S. industries. In one survey of such studies Weiss reported that "the bulk of the studies show a significant, positive effect of concentration on profits or margins . . . the studies together reflect a wide range of experience. . . ."[1] Probably the best-known of these works is Bain's. He hypothesized that this relationship may be due to the opportunities that large firms have for collusion. Bain looked at data for 42 industries from the 1936–1940 period. For the group of "highly concentrated" industries (those with eight-firm concentration ratios in excess of 0.70) the average profit rate was 11.8 percent; for all the others it was only 7.5 percent. Though Bain was careful not to place a great deal of confidence in the limited data that were available, he did note that there seemed to be a significant difference between profit rates for the two classes of industries.[2] A large number of the authors cited by Weiss agreed with Bain that the higher profit figures were probably the result of either outright collusion or a lack of vigorous price competition among the large firms in high-concentration industries. One dissenting voice, however, was that of Yale Brozen. He questioned whether the high profit rates earned by firms in Bain's sample were maintained over time or whether they were temporary. Brozen obtained industry profit figures for Bain's sample, but for the years 1953 to 1957. He found that profit rates regressed towards the mean, with those industries that earned high profits in the earlier period earning lower rates in the 1950. Similarly, the lower profit industries in the earlier period improved their performance in the latter period. Brozen also obtained data for a larger number of industries (eighty) for 1936–1940. Using the larger sample, Brozen claimed that the profit rate differential was not as great as Bain reported.[3]

Still, the large number of studies that show a positive relationship between concentration and profits, however weak or qualified, suggest that it has some validity. If one accepts this, there is at least one explanation other than that which attributes high profits to collusion: firms that have relatively large market shares are more efficient than their competitors. Successful marketing and/or innovation may allow large firms to grow relative to other firms in their industries. Demsetz was among the first to test the proposition that the profit rates of small and large firms in an industry may differ as a result of differences in efficiency. To test this hypothesis Demsetz obtained IRS and *Census of Manufacturers* data for account- ing rates of return (for firms of various sizes in the same industries) and concen- tration ratios. His rationale was that if collusion exists among the largest firms, smaller firms should find shelter underneath a collusive "umbrella"; i.e., these firms will be able to charge the same prices as their larger competitors and earn relatively high rates of return. It was then reasoned that a finding of higher profit rates for the largest firms and lower rates for smaller firms in the same industry would support the "superior efficiency" explanation.[4]

Demsetz presented rate of return data for ninety-five industries, broken into six concentration ranges. These ranges were based on 1963 four-firm concentra- tion ratios for industry sales. Accounting rates of return equaled profit plus in- terest as a percentage of total assets. Two sets of figures were presented, using unweighted data and data weighting rates of return by asset sizes. Both sets are reproduced here in tables 14A and 14B. He then regressed differences in rates of return on concentration (definitions of variables are given in table 14B):[5]

$$R_4 - R_1 = -1.4 + .21 \; C_{63} \qquad\qquad R^2 = .09$$

$$R_4 - R_2 = -2.6 + .12 \; C_{63} \qquad\qquad R^2 = .04$$

$$R_4 - R_3 = -3.1 + .10 \; C_{63} \qquad\qquad R^2 = .04$$

The coefficients of the concentration variable in all three equations were signifi- cant at least at the .05 level.

Demsetz argued that

> The rate of return earned by firms in the smallest asset size does not increase with concentra- tion. . . . The data do not seem to support the notion that concentration and collusion are close- ly related. . . . The regressions reveal a positive relationship between concentration and dif- ferences in rates of return, especially when comparing the largest and smallest firms in an industry.[6]

Demsetz' results were criticized by Bond and Greenberg, who noted that

> among the concentrated industries the average firm in Demsetz' dominant-firm size class is 31 times as large as the average firm in his second-largest size class . . . his comparisons are simply not relevant . . . [7]

Demsetz responded to this by incorporating new, more refined data into a similar study. Examining simple correlations between rates of return and concentration by asset size for 1958, 1963, 1966, 1967, and 1970, he still found that

> larger firms tend to record higher profit rates, and this tendency is stronger in concentrated than in unconcentrated industries. . . . The data are supportive of the belief that there is more to the general correlation between profit rates and concentration than mere collusion.[8]

Table 14A.   1963 Rates of Return for 95 Industries by Size and
Concentration (Unweighted)

$^a C_{63}$	No. of Industries	$^b R_1$	R_2	R_3	R_4	$^c \bar{R}$
10-20%	14	6.5%	9.0%	10.8%	10.3%	9.2%
20-30	22	4.5	9.1	9.7	10.4	8.4
30-40	24	5.2	8.7	9.9	11.0	8.7
40-50	21	5.8	9.0	9.5	9.0	8.3
50-60	11	6.7	9.8	10.5	13.4	10.1
Over 60	3	5.3	10.1	11.5	23.1	12.5

Table 14B.   1963 Rates of Return (Weighted by Assets)

C_{63}	No. of Industries	R_1	R_2	R_3	R_4	$\bar{R}$
10-20%	14	7.3%	9.5%	10.6%	8.0%	8.8%
20-30	22	4.4	8.6	9.9	10.6	8.4
30-40	24	5.1	9.0	9.4	11.7	8.8
40-50	21	4.8	9.5	11.2	9.4	8.7
50-60	11	0.9	9.6	10.8	12.2	8.4
Over 60	3	5.0	8.6	10.3	21.6	11.3

$^a C_{63}$ = four-firm concentration ratio for 1963 industry sales.

$^b R_1$ to R_4 = accounting rates of return for firms with asset values less than
$500,000; $500,000 to $5 million; $5 million to $50 million, and
over $50 million.

$^c \bar{R}$ = unweighted row averages.

Note: Reprinted, by permission of the publisher, from H. Demsetz, "Industry
Structure, Market Rivalry and Public Policy," Journal of Law and Economics,
16 (1973): 6.

A similar pattern was subsequently shown by Demsetz to persist when data for
the 1969–1970 period were used. Table 15 produces his results for correlations between rates of return and concentration ratios. He commented that: "the only
positive correlation between profit rates and concentration is for larger firms, and
there is a suggestion of a negative correlation for smaller firms."[9]
Summarizing his position, Demsetz wrote:

> The competitive view of industry structure suggests that rapid changes in concentration are brought
> about by changed cost conditions and not by alterations in the height of entry barriers. Industries
> experiencing rapid increases in concentration should exhibit greater disparities between large

Table 15. Correlations between Rates of Return[a] and Concentration[b]
(By Asset Size of Firm)
1969 and 1970 Data

Asset Size (Thousands of Dollars)	Correlation Coefficients
Under 10	-.09
10 - 25	-.10
25 - 50	-.40
50 - 100	.00
100 - 250	-.14
250 - 500	-.23
500 - 1,000	-.09
1,000 - 2,500	-.07
2,500 - 5,000	-.27
5,000 - 10,000	.00
10,000 - 25,000	-.06
25,000 - 35,000	-.05
35,000 - 50,000	+.20
50,000 - 100,000	+.05
Over 100,000	+.24

[a]Rate of return = profit before taxes over total assets.

[b]Concentration ratio = four-firm concentration ratio for total sales.

Note: Reprinted, by permission of the publisher, from H. Demsetz, The Market Concentration Doctrine (Washington: American Enterprise Institute, 1973): 25.

and small firm rates of return because of the more significant cost differences which are the root cause of rapid alterations in industry structure.[10]

Peltzman has examined the relationship between concentration and industry costs in more detail. He reasoned that technological change may be responsible for Demsetz' findings. A firm that implemented a new (process) technology would experience a lowering of its average costs; as this happens, the firm would be able to increase its market share. There may well be some downward pressure on price, but it is quite possible that this decline is not so great as to eliminate economic profits. This could be due either to a slow diffusion of the technology to other firms or to the presence of collusion in the now more concentrated industry. In the case of industries with constant returns to scale, where many different firm sizes minimize average costs, implementation of cost-reducing technology may still lead to greater concentration:

> If there is no unique efficient firm size, but only a wide band encompassing many existing firms, then any of these firms can grow to the upper end of the band before it incurs size diseconomies. . . . The potential profits from the cost advantage will then attract capital and permit the firm to grow at least to the upper end of the band, though . . . the firm may also have to reduce prices. Thus, the fortunate firm, or firms, become big instead of merely "average" (concentration increases) and resource costs and prices are lowered by this unusual growth.[11]

One certainly cannot rule out the possibility that relatively small firms can be the innovators. With slow diffusion of new technology, then, declines in concentration can also be correlated with relatively high profit rates. Though such a relationship has not been found to be common (e.g., by Demsetz), Peltzman argued that a model linking market structure to cost changes should allow for the possibility, with its significance subject to empirical verification.

A richer theoretical model, in interpreting Demsetz' results (that rates of return in low-concentration industries tend to be similar for large and small firms while in high-concentration industries returns are greater for larger firms), would not necessarily rule out the possibility of collusion in concentrated industries. As long as one allows for differences in marginal and average costs among firms in an industry, any configuration of concentration and rates of return may be consistent with either the "collusion" or "efficiency" arguments. For example, a collusive agreement among relatively large firms in an industry, all of which have lower average costs than smaller firms, may produce relatively high profits for the large firms. Yet, the smaller firms can survive by charging the collusive price.

Therefore, Peltzman developed a model that attempted to generalize the relationship between market structure and costs. The model begins by assuming that there are two types of firms in an industry: type L are the largest (or those that will grow to be so), and type M are all others. Industry unit cost is then defined to be a weighted average of the unit costs of both firm types:

(1) $C = sL + (1 - s)M$

s = output share of the larger firms (e.g., a four-firm concentration ratio)

L = unit cost of output for the larger firms

M = unit cost of output for the other firms

Peltzman differentiated this equation with respect to time. He assumed that changes in market structure were related to cost differences between the two firm groups; the type of firm with a cost advantage would grow faster over time in proportion to its cost advantage. Also, he noted that some empirical studies had shown a negative correlation between changes in concentration and market growth:

> In a model which purports to link market structure to differential costs, such an empirical regularity must logically be cost related . . . assume that rapid growth reduces the small-firm cost change relative to that of large firms . . . [12]

To test his model Peltzman performed a three-term Taylor expansion of the cost change equation to obtain:

(1') $$\dot{C} = r + \text{ags} + bg(1 - s) + (b - a)g \left[\frac{Z^2 M_j}{\alpha_i^2 K_i} - \frac{ZM_i}{\alpha_i} \right]$$
$$- \frac{-Z^2}{\alpha_i s(1 - s)} + \text{Remainder}$$

where: $\dot{C}$ = industry unit cost change over time

r = the sum of all forces changing costs which are common to all firms

a, b = forces that change costs and are peculiar to large and small firms, respectively; a and b are constants

g = market growth

$z = ds/dt$ = absolute value of the change in concentration

$\alpha_1, \alpha_2 > 0$, and are constants

$K_1 = s, K_2 = (1 - s)$

$M_1 = -1, M_2 = 1$

Equation (1') is used to represent situations of increased concentration (ds/dt exceeds zero and i = 1) and decreased concentration (ds/dt is less than zero and i = 2). Peltzman used three cost-share-weighted input price change variables to estimate r. If growth is advantageous for small firms, (b − a) should be negative. To summarize the model, then, the rate of industry cost change ($\dot{C}$) is related to the level of industry concentration (s), the change in concentration (Z), and the rate of industry growth. Cost changes are linked to changes in concentration by the assumption that increases (decreases) in concentration are proportional to the cost advantage (disadvantage) of large firms over small firms. The proportionality constant is α_i. The growth of market share by the more efficient firms reduces industry unit costs.

Peltzman tested his hypothesis that changes in industry costs (and, therefore, efficiency) can be explained by changes in market structure by selecting a group of 165 four-digit Standard Industrial Classification (SIC) manufacturing industries. Data were obtained for the 1947 and 1967 years. Other industries were left out of his sample due to the noncomparability or nonavailability of data for the two years:

> . . . industries had to be dropped because of changes in classification between 1947 and 1967, or because reliable output indexes were unavailable from 1947. To limit potential measurement error, industries with low or changing coverage or specialization ratios were also deleted.[13]

Specifically, Peltzman left out industries whose coverage or specialization ratios (these measure the degree to which firms classified in one industry engage in production in this industry relative to others) were under 0.6 or where either changed by over 0.1 between the two years. Table 16 shows the distribution of Peltzman's sample of industries by their two-digit classification.

To test his model, Peltzman found empirical counterparts to the variables in equation (1'), and he regressed unit cost changes on the independent variables of the equation (see table 17). In its *Census of Manufacturers*, the Bureau of the Census publishes four-digit indexes of production. These indexes have been designed to provide measures of the change in the value of work done in establishments, classified in each industry, valued in constant dollars to eliminate the effects of price changes. Deflating total costs (equal to labor plus capital plus raw materials expenditures for each year) by production indexes for his sample of industries, Peltzman derived his estimates for unit costs. Percentage changes in industry unit costs were then computed (using natural logs) for 1947 and 1967. The cost data were also available from the *Census of Manufacturers*. Peltzman computed cost-share-weighted price changes for the three inputs;[14] cost shares used were averages for the two years. To compute input price changes, the following variables were used: (1) payroll per employee, for the price of labor; (2) an index which estimated for each industry the direct and indirect purchases of

Table 16. Breakdown of Peltzman's Industry Sample
(1958 SIC Classification)

Industry	Two-digit SIC Number	Number of Four-digit Industries in Peltzman's Sample
Food and Kindred	20	21
Tobacco Manufacturers	21	3
Textile Mill Products	22	9
Apparel and Related Products	23	13
Lumber and Wood Products	24	4
Furniture and Fixtures	25	4
Pulp, Paper and Products	26	5
Printing and Publishing	27	11
Chemicals and Products	28	6
Petroleum and Coal Products	29	2
Rubber Products	30	3
Leather and Leather Goods	31	6
Stone, Clay and Glass	32	15
Primary Metal Industries	33	6
Fabricated Metal Products	34	10
Machinery, except Electrical	35	11
Electrical Machinery	36	13
Transportation Equipment	37	7
Instruments and Related Products	38	3
Miscellaneous Manufacturing	39	13
Total		165

Source: Correspondence from S. Peltzman.

agricultural products per dollar of purchases;[15] (3) a constant cost-share-weighted price variable, since no disaggregated capital price data were available by industry.

The market share variables were estimated with four-firm concentration ratios, also published by the *Census of Manufacturers*. Therefore, z was set equal to the absolute value of the change in each industry's concentration ratio; and the market shares of the small and large firms (s and $1 - s$), respectively, were the averages of these ratios for the two years. To compute g, the estimate of demand or output growth, the log of 1967 divided by 1947 sales minus the log change in the manufactured goods wholesale price index was taken for each industry.

To compute α_1 and α_2, Peltzman regressed the dependent variable on the components of the CR1 variable (a separate regression was run for industries experienc-

Table 17.   Regression of Unit Cost Changes on Market Structure Variables, 1947–1967[a]

		Independent Variables	Coefficient	t-Statistic
		Input Cost Share (ai)x Input Price Changes (pi)		
1.	LAB	i = labor	1.211	4.639
2.	RMT	i = raw materials	.911	1.480
3.	CAP	i = capital (cost share only)	.980	2.053
		Growth in Demand:		
4.	G1	gs	.079	.901
5.	G2	g(1-s)	.116	2.150
		Change in Concentration:		
6.	CR1+	$g[\dfrac{z^2_{Mi}}{\alpha^2_i K_i} - \dfrac{z_{Mi}}{\alpha_i}]$, For increases in concentration (zero otherwise)	-2.245	-3.245
7.	CR2+	$\alpha \dfrac{z^2}{is(1-s)}$, for increases in concentration (0 otherwise) [α_1 = .856 for (6) and (7)]	- .006	- .026
8.	CR1-	Same as (6), for decreases in concentration	- .645	-1.546
9.	CR2-	Same as (7), decreases in concentration [α_2 = -1.046 for (8) and (9)]	- .484	-1.006
Constant Term			- .328	-1.686
R^2		Coefficient of Determination	.342	
SE		Regression Standard Error x 100	20.760	

[a]The Dependent Variable is the log difference in unit costs for 1967 and 1947.

Note: Reprinted, by permission of the author, from S. Peltzman, "The Gains and Losses from Industrial Concentration," *Journal of Law and Economics*, 20 (1977): 246.

ing increases and decreases in concentration; see table 17) and divided the coefficient of the variable's second term by the coefficient of the first term. The resulting least squares estimates for α_1 and α_2 minimize residual variance. The negative value of α_2 seemed implausible to Peltzman, but he reported that assuming values for α_1 and α_2 ranging from -30 to $+30$ resulted in only trivial variation in the explanatory power of the regression.

To test whether increases in concentration had a significant effect on cost changes, and whether this effect was greater than for decreases in concentration, Peltzman used two sets of CR1 and CR2 variables to represent the effects for each of these subgroups.[16] In summarizing his results, Peltzman noted that: (a) as implied by the model, the first two factor price variables were insignificantly different from +1; (b) there was not the expected difference between large and small firm cost changes. That is, the coefficient of G2 was not less than that of G1; (c) contrary to expectations, CR1 was not equal to the difference between the G2 and G1 coefficients.

Peltzman recognized that the model may have been misspecified, but he still claimed that there was a decided difference between increases and decreases in concentration in terms of their effects on unit costs. Moreover, these results were consistent with Demsetz' hypothesis: decreases in concentration did seem to reduce costs, but the strongest influence came from the CR1 variable. Increases in concentration in slow-growing markets had no significant effect on costs, but increases in concentration in growing markets had the greatest impact on cost changes of any of the market structure variables.

As a test of the model's specification, another regression was run with the CR1 and CR2 variables replaced by four linear terms: linear growth interaction terms (gZ) and concentration ratios (s) were entered separately for industries experiencing increases and decreases in concentration (i.e., two gZ and two s terms were used). The results were similar to those of the more complex regression, with R^2 virtually the same (=.33) and the coefficients gZ and s significantly negative for increases in concentration and insignificantly negative for decreases in concentration.

Peltzman addressed a critical issue in the study when he considered the length of the period used for his analysis. Firms may expand by moving along a single cost curve or by expanding along a new (lower) cost curve subsequent to a change in technology. The distinction is crucial since it is the latter that is supposed to be captured:

> Over the short periods, concentration changes will be dominated by forces—like differences between the shape of large and small firm short-run marginal costs—which are ignored by our theory. Moreover, firms which are expanding rapidly to take advantage of their lower long-run costs can incur a short-run adjustment cost penalty. All this suggests that if we focus on too short a time period, the market structure-cost relationship will be unreliable and attenuated.[17]

The definition of a "short" period is obviously arbitrary, so Peltzman ran similar regressions for various subperiods. He did not report the full regression results, but he did note that for three periods (1947–1963, 1954–1967, 1947–58) the coefficient of the CR1+ variable: (a) was significant (with t-statistics all in excess of 2.0) and negative; (b) showed a greater reduction in cost than CR1− for each subperiod; (c) was less than the CR1+ coefficient for the 1947–1967 period.   Summarizing these results, he wrote:

> The general pattern observed in the full period tends to hold for the subperiods. Changes in concentration are associated with cost reductions, and they are more pronounced when concentration increases. However, the subperiod effects tend to be smaller than the full period effects. This indicates that the . . . process generating cost reductions takes . . . time . . . to work itself out.[18]

Peltzman used the results from his model in order to make a contribution to the "collusion versus efficiency" interpretation of the studies that linked high concentration to high profitability. Generally, he finds that the efficiency effects of changes in concentration outweigh the price effects. This part of his study, however, is not of primary interest here; it is his market structure model, and the empirical implications he derives from it, that are of interest.

Cost and Concentration Changes: What Peltzman's Results Show

The model that Peltzman used to explain industry cost changes is what he refers to as a "natural oligopoly" theory. Peltzman used a graph similar to that of figure 2 to illustrate this theory.[19] In the graph DD′ represents the demand for a homogeneous product in what is initially a competitive industry. The long-run supply (marginal cost) curve of the industry is P_1C_1. Peltzman assumed that, since constant returns to scale have been often observed in studies of U.S. industries, the firm's long-run supply curve is P_1RM. Therefore, actual firm size is indeterminate within the range of output OQ_2. Suppose that the actual firm output is OQ_3, and a four-firm concentration ratio of $4(OQ_3/OQ_1)$ was observed. The industry would be in equilibrium with zero economic profits and a price of P_1. Now assume that one firm discovered a new production method that cut its marginal cost to P_2NRM. The firm is assumed to expand to the outer boundary of this curve so that its output would increase to OQ_2. The firm would earn short-run profits and industry concentration would increase (by Q_3Q_2/OQ_1). There is a cost saving of P_1P_2NR, part of which ($Q_3Q_2 \times NR$) is realized through the increase in concentration.

Ultimately, one may observe all firms implementing the new production method so that the long-run industry supply curve shifts to P_2C_2. Economic profits will be positive as long as the new technology is being diffused, though in long-run equilibrium they will be eliminated. Depending on how elastic the demand for this product is, industry concentration may either be greater or less than it was originally. "But, given the very large maximal sizes usually encountered in the scale economies literature, increased concentration would be the expected outcome."[20] Peltzman then concluded that

> where differences in firms' costs underlie changes in their market shares, one ought to expect any change in market structure to promote efficiency. However, with constant returns-to-scale, there is a clear bias toward increased concentration as the main source of lower costs. So long as a firm's superior technology simply lowers the level of its horizontal marginal cost curve, the firm will expand to maximal efficient size.[21]

It is interesting to note that the "natural oligopoly" model places great emphasis on technological change as the source of cost and concentration changes. Yet, the model is applied to a competitive industry within which a homogeneous output is produced. As was noted in chapter 1, the difficulty of appropriating the

Figure 2

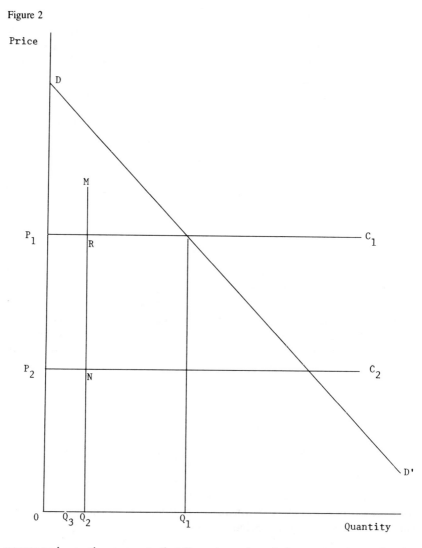

returns to innovation suggests that firms in such an industry may be unlikely to engage in very much R and D. What Peltzman suggests is that firms "stumble onto" new cost-reducing techniques, rather than going out to search for them.[22] Should innovation be the result of private investments in R and D, the competitive market assumption would seem inappropriate. Nelson and Winter, although not in response to Peltzman's work, recognized the roles that R and D and appropriability can play in influencing industry cost patterns.[23] Figure 3 illustrates an industry with the product demand curve DD'. A key feature of this model is a gap between the marginal cost and price of the most efficient firms in the industry. In addition,

Figure 3

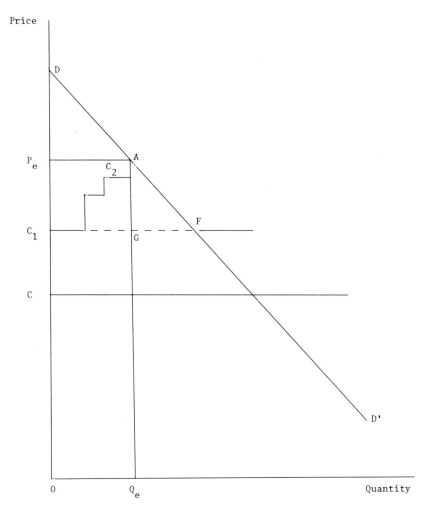

it is assumed that a firm can appropriate the returns to new technology investments (via patents, trade secrets, etc.). These assumptions imply that there are two types of costs associated with limitations on access by all firms to new technology. The first cost is due to a gap between the most efficient production methods ("best practice") and less efficient methods ("average practice"). Another cost is that associated with duplicative R and D efforts. In other words, more R and D spending is undertaken in order to establish a given best practice technique than would be spent if all firms had immediate access to all new technology.[24]

    In figure 3, OC represents the marginal and average costs that would result if all firms in the industry employed best practice techniques, while C_1C_2 traces the actual cost schedule for the industry, ranging from the unit cost of the most efficient firm(s), or C_1, to that of the least efficient firms (C_2). In this example potential consumers' surplus is equal to DCB, but the actual surplus is only DC_1C_2A. The difference between the areas is equal to the sum of: (a) the dead weight loss (AFG) associated with lower output at Q_e than would be produced with best practice techniques, and (b) the excess production costs due to the difference between best practice and average practice (C_1C_2G), and (c) the lower best practice due to inefficient industry R and D (CC_1FB). Of course, to encourage firms to undertake R and D projects, some of these costs must be paid.[25]

Still another issue raised with the use of the "natural oligopoly" theory is the identification of technological change with cost reductions (i.e., discovery of new or improved processes). Yet, the majority of private R and D is devoted to the development of new products.[26] The effect of product innovation is to alter the demand for the innovator's output. Should this occur, the measurement of "industry output" becomes problematical. In fact, Peltzman recognizes this difficulty, although his model does not distinguish between product and process innovation. Peltzman wrote that two industries (drugs and ball point pens) had to be dropped from his sample because they "experienced profound technological change . . . their measured productivity growth was so atypical as to obscure some of the results and raise questions about the comparability of the earlier and later outputs."[27]

Scherer observed that, in spite of Peltzman's attempts to purge his sample of unrepresentative industries, most of the industries in his sample that had experienced the greatest increases in concentration for 1947 to 1967 were consumer goods industries (i.e., they sold most of their outputs to consumers rather than other producers), not producer goods industries (see table 18).[28] Surveys have shown that product innovation is more likely to occur within consumer goods industries, while there is a greater propensity for process innovation among producer goods industries.[29]

In his own analysis of 154 four-digit industries, Scherer found that between 1947 and 1972 four-firm concentration ratios had fallen (by an average of 1.7 percentage points) among 87 industries classified as producer goods industries (i.e., those that sold less than 33 percent of their outputs to consumers) but had risen (by an average of 6.4 percentage points) among consumer goods industries (those that sold over 60 percent of their outputs to consumers).[30] Of course, in analyzing changes in concentration over time, one realizes that some industries will experience increased or reduced concentration as the result of random or transitory factors that may later be reversed. If this were the sole explanation for changed concentration, however, one would find more of a random distribution of producer and consumer goods industries among the increased and decreased concentration samples.

Table 18. Characteristics of Industries with High 1947–1967
Concentration Changes

1958 SIC	Industry Description	Change in Concentration 1947–67	Consumer Demand as % of Total Demand
3633	Household Laundry Equipment	+38	82 (c)
2771	Greeting Card Publishing	+28	82 (c)
3421	Cutlery	+28	66 (c)
3872	Watchcases	+28	n.a. (p)
3263	Fine Earthenware Food Utensils	+23	52 (c)
3717	Motor Vehicles and Parts	+22	55 (c)
3229	Pressed and Blown Glass	+20	n.a. (p)
2082	Beer Brewing	+19	83 (c)
2121	Cigars	+18	96 (c)
3121	Industrial Leather Belting	+18	n.a. (p)
2087	Flavoring Extracts and Syrups	+17	37 (p)
3555	Printing Trades Machinery	+17	0 (p)
2073	Chewing Gum	+16	89 (c)
3554	Paper Industries Machinery	+15	0 (p)
3751	Motorcycles and Bicycles	+15	75 (c)
2342	Corsets and Allied Garments	+14	n.a. (c)
3262	Vitreous China Food Utensils	+14	52 (c)
3953	Marking Devices	+14	n.a. (p)

Source: F. M. Scherer, "The Causes and Consequences of Rising Industrial Concentration," Journal of Law and Economics, 22 (1979): 194.

Note: Letters in parentheses indicate whether an industry is classified as a consumer goods (c) or producer goods (p) industry.

For another group of 323 four-digit SIC manufacturing industries, table 19 shows average values of several market structure variables. For the 1958 to 1972 time period, the table also presents average values for industries that experienced increased and decreased concentration (industries that experienced no change in concentration were included in both subsamples). As Scherer found with his data, there are clear differences between the two subsamples. Statistical tests indicated that there are significant differences between the means of industry wages (for 1958), research intensity (1962), the 1963 percentage of industry output sold to

Table 19. Descriptive Statistics for U.S. Industries

Variable	All Industries (323)		Industries with Decreased Concentration from 1958-1972 (213)		Industries with Increased Concentration from 1958-1972 (122)	
	Mean	(Standard Deviation)	Mean	(Standard Deviation)	Mean	(Standard Deviation)
Wage	$ 2.11	(0.46)	$ 2.18	(0.42)	$ 2.01	(0.51)
RES	3.01	(3.11)	3.36	(3.20)	2.36	(2.74)
CONS	0.27	(0.34)	0.21	(0.31)	0.36	(0.36)
K/L	11.04	(12.02)	11.91	(12.68)	9.50	(10.34)
VA	325.08	(518.37)	354.04	(556.72)	282.55	(462.42)

Notes: Wage is equal to industry wage rate per-worker per-man-hour for 1958. RES equals 1962 industry R and D spending divided by total sales. CONS is the 1963 percentage of industry output sold to consumers. K/L equals the industry capital-labor ratio for 1964. VA is industry value-added for 1958.

consumers (all at the 0.01 level), and 1964 capital-labor ratios (at the 0.10 level). Additional data for this sample were obtained for 103 increased concentration (IC) industries and 77 decreased concentration (DC) industries; 12 industries that experienced no change in concentration were included in both of these subsamples. The data indicated that the average annual growth of output (measured by the log change of industry production indexes),[31] and the average levels of concentration (the simple average of the four-firm concentration ratios for 1958 and 1972), were greater for the DC industries, although the differences were not statistically significant.

That there are differences between the IC and DC industries is quite clear. Scherer suggests that "there must be some difference in the structural-change dynamics associated with the types of buyer."[32] He regressed the change in the four-firm concentration ratios of the 154 industries in his sample on several market structure variables and found "concentration rose significantly more rapidly in consumer goods industries and in industries with relatively high advertising expenditures."[33] These results suggest that the relationship between technological change and concentration is more complex than is suggested by the "natural oligopoly" theory. The data may also be related to Comanor's examination of product differentiation and the propensity for industry R and D.

> In industries where products are differentiable, and where as a result, competitiveness in research is an important element of market behavior, it may be that concentration is not a significant factor. Where, however, product differentiation is less important, concentration is more likely to play a major role. In the latter area, research programs are more likely to emphasize the development of new processes or techniques of production. While these may be important, they should have fewer competitive consequences than in industries where the development of new products is a major source of rivalry. In these industries, the neo-Schumpeterian hypothesis that a positive relationship exists between concentration and industrial research may well be correct.[34]

The IC industries referred to in tables 18 and 19 are generally less concentrated and less capital-intensive than the DC industries. Although consumer and producer goods industries are present among the DC subsample, there is a greater consumer goods orientation among firms in the IC subsample, and an apparently greater propensity for product differentiation (due, in part, to product innovation). These results, coupled with Comanor's finding, indicate that product differentiation may have been responsible for the expansion of the market shares of relatively large firms among the IC industries during the periods covered.

The difference in research intensity between the IC and DC industries represents another challenge to Peltzman's results. If privately financed R and D had been responsible for cost-reducing, concentration-increasing technological change, one would expect to find the research intensity of IC industries to be greater than that of the DC industries.[35] The research data referred to in table 19 are highly aggregated and do not specify the type of research that industries carry out (e.g., basic versus applied or process versus product). Nevertheless, in order to accept the "natural oligopoly" explanation for Peltzman's results, one would have to explain why, inter alia, despite lower average spending on R and D, IC industries (at least those that experienced rapid growth) had been prone to substantial cost-reducing technological change (possibly due to random, scale-increasing discoveries?). It is not clear how such an explanation would square with the data presented above.

At least two other alternative explanations for Peltzman's results may be suggested. First, the model he used to estimate his theory was misspecified. Second, the cost reductions he observed may be due to something other than technological change. Lustgarten pointed to several problems that arose from the specification of Peltzman's model. As table 17 shows, the brunt of Peltzman's results depends upon an interaction between market growth and concentration. In fact, market growth appears in so many of the variables that its influence dominates the results. In this structure, it is impossible to determine the independent effect of any of the market structure variables.

Lustgarten revised and simplified Peltzman's model and tested it with data from another time period (1954–1972).[36] He used a measure of the (negative) growth in total factor productivity as an estimate of industry cost change (154 industries were in the sample). This variable equals the change in unit costs that would have occurred in the absence of factor price changes. Lustgarten then assumed that the growth rates of unit costs for large and small firms are equal (b = a in equation 1′). This allows the interaction term (growth and concentration change) to be eliminated from the model. Peltzman assumed that industry growth led to a dynamic cost advantage for small firms since many empirical studies found rapid growth to be correlated with declines in concentration. Lustgarten argued, however, that concentration could be reduced by: (a) entry of smaller and less efficient firms in response to higher prices or (b) expansion by existing firms that previously were at less than optimal scale. The former possibility is consistent with cost increases, while the latter implies that unit costs would decline as growth takes place. Assuming equality between small and large firm unit cost growth, equation (1′) can be simplified as follows:[37]

$$(1') \quad \dot{C} = r + ag - Z^2/ \, \alpha s \, (1 - s)$$

Table 20 shows the results from the regression of unit cost changes on g and $Z^2/s \, (1 - s)$. The constant term is the estimate for r, and the coefficient of the growth variable is the estimate for a. Note that the coefficient of the market structure variable, $Z^2/s \, (1 - s)$, is equal to $-1/\alpha$. Therefore, the estimates of α_1 and α_2 are equal to the negative inverse of the coefficients of these variables in table 20. Note that Lustgarten, like Peltzman, bifurcates the market structure variable in order to derive separate estimates for industries with increased and decreased

Table 20. Regression Estimates of Changes in Concentration on Changes in Unit Cost, 1954–72 (159 Four-Digit SIC Industries)

	Modified Peltzman Model			General Linear Model	
Variable	Coefficient	t-Statistic	Variable	Coefficient	t-Statistic
Constant	.078	1.43	Constant	.228	1.97
g	-.286	12.39	g	-.304	7.36
$Z^2 \cdot D_1 / s(1-s)$	-.961	2.90	D_1	-.004	.05
$Z^2 \cdot D_2 / s(1-s)$	1.402	2.57	$D_1 \cdot Z$	-.019	2.46
$\bar{R}^2$	.495		$D_2 \cdot Z$	.008	.60
SEE	.325		$D_1 \cdot Z \cdot g$	.004	1.10
			$D_2 \cdot Z \cdot g$	.001	.11
			s	-.002	1.78
			$\bar{R}^2$	.495	
			SEE	.326	

Note: Dependent variable is the negative of the change in total factor productivity.

Z = concentration change

D_1 = 1 for concentration increases and zero otherwise.

D_2 = 1 for concentration decreases and zero otherwise.

g = real output growth; s = average level of concentration.

Reprinted, by permission of author, from S. Lustgarten, "Gains and Losses from Concentration: A Comment," Journal of Law and Economics, 22 (1979): 187.

concentration. The coefficients for all of the independent variables are significant, and the estimates of α_1 and α_2 are 1.04 and $-.713$, respectively. Lustgarten summarized his results as follows:

> Both increasing and decreasing concentration have statistically significant impacts on unit costs, but the former is associated with relative decreases in cost while the latter with relative increases. . . . Peltzman also observed a negative value for α_2, but discounted its significance . . .
>
> However, . . . the negative value should not be ignored. It implies that decreasing concentration should be interpreted as . . . distinctly different and opposite in terms of its impact on costs from increasing concentration.[38]

Lustgarten suggested that the negative value for α_2 implies that decreases in concentration are due to entry of less efficient firms and that cost-saving innovations seldom cause reductions in minimum efficient firm size. Note too that the results show a significant effect for the concentration variable; this is true both for the simplified Peltzman model and Lustgarten's linear model (though for the latter model only increases in concentration are significantly related to cost changes).

Although Lustgarten's results supported the thrust of Peltzman's work with respect to the effects of increased concentration, the results he obtained for decreased concentration industries were different. Lustgarten then examined the effects of concentration on prices and profits. He found that the cost reduction effect of increased concentration outweighed any tendency for higher prices and that both higher unit costs and prices resulted from decreased concentration. Finally, he noted that the "hypothesis offered here is closer to the traditional notion that the level of industry concentration is a function of the degree of economies of scale and the size of the market."[39]

Scherer also attributed Peltzman's results to economies of scale (which could be plant-specific or product-specific).

> . . . there is almost sure to be a period of rapid unit cost decline as the bugs are worked out of production techniques and as further product design changes are made. . . . The rate of process improvement is likely to attenuate as the product technology matures, and so one would expect to see unit costs fall more rapidly in industries with a relatively turbulent product technology, all else equal.[40]

However, the consumer goods orientation of the IC industries makes the task of measuring unit cost changes, the dependent variable in Peltzman's regressions, difficult. This is especially true since firms will often produce in several product areas. The production indexes used in the construction of unit cost changes often do not adequately capture the effect of the introduction of new products. This will be especially true for a new product whose quality or durability is markedly different from a similar, but older, product. For example, suppose that a firm introduced a new widget that had twice the useful life of an older version. Assume that the total number of widgets sold one year after the new widget was first introduced was the same as the number sold the previous year, with old and new widgets dividing the market equally. In one sense, the output of widgets is exactly the same in both years; but clearly, the total utility received by consumers of the widgets sold in the second year will exceed the utility derived from the first year's widgets. The revenue received by producers would depend on the price charged for the two types of output. It is this revenue that would be deflated by a price index in order to derive the output index for each year. Only if the price of the new widget were twice as high as the old price would the output index accurately reflect the increase in the quality of the widgets produced. However, the output of widgets, from the standpoint of the firm, has not changed; only if the price were the same for both types of widgets would the index accurately measure output in this sense. Clearly, a number of different outcomes are possible. Should product innovation result in an entirely different new product, the interpretation of the output indexes would become even more problematical.

Still, Scherer claimed that a relationship between rising concentration and unit cost declines may be expected.

> It is . . . likely that with a rapid pace of product innovation, the unit costs of producing any given product variant decline by a relatively large amount over time . . . it is reasonable to suppose that a favorable "learning curve" manifests itself at least [with respect to] . . . total cost. . . . To the extent that process improvement is correlated with the product innovation, which in turn is correlated with rising concentration, regression of unit cost changes on a concentration variable will correctly reveal a negative relationship.[41]

Peltzman responded to Scherer's criticisms by backing away somewhat from the "natural oligopoly" theory.

> Professor Scherer has misread my criticism of an exclusive focus on an economies of scale explanation of market structure as a wholesale dismissal of their importance . . . the model . . . can easily comprehend Scherer's insistence on the importance of scale economics [*sic*]. The most general statement of the model is simply that more efficient firms will tend to grow faster than others. If the source of that efficiency [is] scale economies rather than a lowered horizontal cost curve, the net result is the same: increased concentration and increased efficiency.[42]

The emphasis given to economies of scale and the learning effects associated with rising concentration by Scherer and Lustgarten is suggestive of the "experience curve" strategies formulated by management consultants during the 1960s. The Boston Consulting Group is credited with popularizing the concept of the experience curve as a corporate strategy (although the logic behind it was not anything new)[43] after observing that unit costs had fallen in many industries as the total volume of output increased. From this observation came a recommendation to the Boston Consulting Group's clients: to maximize profits a firm should "drive down" the experience curve by increasing market share. This would simultaneously reduce unit costs and discourage would-be competitors, since it would be difficult for latecomers to overcome the first firm's cost advantage.[44]

Although the experience curve has had useful applications in some instances, its applicability for many industries is limited. It is most appropriate for a firm that produces a single homogeneous product. Should the strategy be applied to a diversified firm, it may be difficult to allocate the firm's costs to individual products. In addition, the theory implies that the path to high profitability lies in high output volume; but many firms survive (or thrive) by targeting their marketing efforts towards a narrow range of consumers. The producers of Molson and Heineken beer have been successful in competition with the market share leaders in the United States (Budweiser and Miller Lite), even though their prices are higher. This has occurred at the same time that many other breweries have been driven out of business, unable either to achieve the market share necessary to minimize average costs or to differentiate their products.

The experience curve and economies of scale may have less to do with interfirm differences in efficiency and profits in consumer goods industries than other sources (e.g., product differentiation and managerial efficiency). In fact, the relationship that Peltzman found (large reductions in unit costs in increased concentration, consumer goods industries) could be the result of a combination of factors.

> Superiority can take several forms. So far as cost-superiority goes, some firms can produce more cheaply than their rivals for some ranges of output, but not for all. . . . Such partial or full cost-superiority can occur even when there are not economies of size in the conventional sense: unit costs of firms may be lower whether the relevant cost functions are U-shaped, decreasing or constant. . . . One management rightly concludes that unit costs can be lowered drastically by producing much larger outputs. Another concludes, wrongly, that there is no such advantage. The performance of the first firm proves to be vastly superior . . . .
>
> Some firms are superior in offering products that consumers value more highly relative to what they cost to produce.[45]

To take McGee's argument one step further, within a given industry two firms with access to the same production techniques may differ in terms of their profitability because one is better managed than the other. It is often found that the most successful firms are those that motivate their employees to share the firms' mission and goals and provide their customers with good service. Economists are often guilty of ignoring these attributes, perhaps due to the difficulty of quantifying them. Nevertheless, there can be no doubt of their importance. Peters and Waterman found these characteristics to be common among the U.S. corporations they identified as especially successful.[46] In fact, they found evidence that economies of scale, at the plant level, had relatively little to do with corporate success.

> We find that the lion's share of the top performers keep their division size between $50 and $100 million, with a maximum of 1,000 or so employees each. Moreover, they grant their divisions extraordinary independence. . . .

For us, the story on plant size was nothing short of astonishing. Repeatedly, we found that the better performers had determined that their small plants, not their big ones, were most efficient. . . .

The conclusion we draw from all of this can be defined as a rough guideline. Regardless of industry, it seems that more than 500 or so people under one roof causes substantial and unanticipated problems. More significant, even for the cost-oriented companies, small is not only more innovative but also more productive.[47]

Most of the companies that Peters and Waterman surveyed are not "small" in either a relative or absolute sense (e.g., Procter & Gamble, IBM, Delta Airlines). In other words, it is not the efficiency conferred by large size per se that they claim is the source of corporate excellence, but the manner in which the firms' resources, regardless of their size, are organized.

The interaction between market growth and increased concentration that Peltzman found led to significant cost reductions may also be explained via a "capital vintage" effect that occurs as the result of a technological advance. In a study of firms in the steel and petroleum industries, Mansfield found that "in the period immediately before they introduced the innovations, there was no persistent tendency for the successful innovator to grow more rapidly than other comparable firms."[48] The average annual growth of firms that carried out significant innovations in his sample period was compared to the corresponding growth rates of other firms of sizes comparable to the innovators.

There is a marked difference between the two groups. In every time interval and in both industries, the successful innovators grew more rapidly than the others; and in some cases their growth rate was more than twice that of the others.

When each innovator is considered separately, the difference between its growth rate and the average growth rate of other comparable firms seems to have been inversely related to its size. As one would expect, a successful innovation had a much greater impact on the growth rate of a small firm than on that of a large firm.[49]

If the latest advances in technology are embedded in the newest plant and equipment ("best practice" techniques), then rapid growth of output will probably mean an increase in productivity as new plants are built. At any one time a firm will utilize any number of plants of various sizes. The average productivity of a firm (or industry) is, then, a weighted average of various plants, with older plants embodying older technology. The older plants will still be used as long as they generate enough revenue to cover their operating costs (the capital costs will be sunk costs). A rapid growth of output will be associated with relatively high rates of new investment in new capacity and a concentration of output in newer plants. As a result, there will be a tendency for overall average productivity to improve and unit costs to fall.[50]

In conclusion, the results that Peltzman (and later Lustgarten) obtained from the tests of his model, and the other evidence presented in this chapter, suggest that the effects (and possibly the causes) of changes in concentration may be different for industries that experience increased, rather than decreased, concentration. However, the attribution of these effects to cost-reducing technological change seems highly questionable. Perhaps the most interesting challenge to this explanation (the "natural oligopoly" theory) is based on the profile of industries that have experienced increased and decreased concentration in the past; the former group of industries are apparently more likely to be consumer goods industries with, on average, a stronger propensity for product differentiation than the latter group. Another difficulty with Peltzman's approach is that the role of R and D is ignored, even though there is ample evidence that productivity growth, and the change in unit costs, across firms and industries is affected by R and D. Although it is difficult to distinguish the sources of cost and productivity change over time (technological change, economies of scale, managerial efficiency, etc.), the evidence presented in this chapter suggests that it would be useful to investigate the role that R and D has had, and whether its effects vary between increased and decreased concentration industries.

5

Research, Productivity, and Concentration: Empirical Analysis

Previous chapters have examined the role that private research and development has in influencing industry structure. Magee sought to establish a dynamic relationship between research intensity and both large firm size and industry structure. Large multinational firms (specifically those from the United States) are seen as specialists in the development of new products and processes. The firms recognize the public good nature of successful resarch efforts and the likely loss of appropriability of the returns to new technology. This recognition influences the type of resarch they conduct and induces them to develop methods of protecting their research investments (e.g., via the use of trade secrets and transfer of new technology to foreign markets through controlled subsidiaries). Successful research increases firm size and industry concentration, and greater concentration lends itself to greater appropriability. However, over time the returns to new research wane and research intensity and concentration lessen.

Much of Magee's argument is intuitively appealing, and there is empirical support for some of his positions (especially his explanation for the choice of transfer vehicle for new technology). However, his industry technology cycle places a great deal of emphasis on research intensity as an explanation for industry concentration and optimal firm size. The tests of the technology cycle that used cross-section data for concentration, industry age, and research failed to capture the cycle's dynamic dimensions. Use of time-series data, however, also presents conceptual and practical difficulties; perhaps the most fundamental problem is that concentration may vary widely across industries for reasons not directly related to research intensity.

Magee's work is suggestive of Schumpeter's claim that some degree of monopoly power is necessary for a high rate of technological innovation. What the empirical tests of this hypothesis show is that large firm size, or industry concentration, is only weakly related to research intensity or technological output and that these relationships vary widely across industries. Comanor, for example, found that industry research and concentration were less highly correlated among industries characterized by high product differentiation than among industries with low levels of product differentiation. Mansfield discovered that although scale-increasing product and process innovations have been more common within several industries than scale-decreasing innovations (in the years since 1920), there was little evidence of a correlation between the extent of scale-increasing innovation and either productivity change or research intensity. Perhaps the most compelling lessons to be learned from these studies are that there is no simple link between research and market structure and that these relationships are likely to be different for different industries.

The works of Demsetz, Peltzman, and Lustgarten examined the effects of changes in concentration on unit costs and profitability. Although their approaches were somewhat different, they all interpreted their results in a similar manner: increased concentration is associated with reduced industry unit costs as relatively large firms increase their market shares. On the other hand, reduced industry concentration appeared to be associated with either much lower cost reductions or increases in industry unit costs. Further analysis by Scherer, and from chapter 4 (table 19), showed that there appear to be differences between increased and decreased concentration industries that may help explain these results. Indeed, several explanations may be given for the apparent differences in cost changes found for increased and decreased concentration industries.

Peltzman's hypothesis that changes in industry unit costs over time may be due, at least in part, to technological change suggests that privately financed R and D should be considered as an explanatory variable. Another question may then be addressed: does R and D have effects on market structure and costs that differ between increased and decreased concentration industries? The profile of firms that have experienced increased concentration in the recent past indicates that product differentiation, perhaps due in part to new product innovation, may have been one reason for the ability of large firms either to increase or to maintain their market shares.

The effect of research effort on the growth of industry output and productivity often has been explored with the use of a production function that has among its explanatory variables a measure of R and D. This same approach will be employed later in this chapter. The approach, though not without conceptual and empirical difficulties, is the best way to estimate the contribution of R and D to growth in a comprehensive manner. Before the empirical results obtained for the model are presented, it will be useful to review some of the inherent problems associated with estimation of the impact of R and D. The following section borrows heavily from Griliches' excellent exposition of these problems.[1]

Measuring the Impact of R and D

Conventional production function analysis is designed to explain changes in output (at a microeconomic or macroeconomic level) as the result of changes in the use of scarce inputs. Historically, short-run production functions have assumed that technological change is given and fixed. As was noted in chapter 1, however, it is useful to think of technological change as an independent variable over which firms have some control (at least in the long run) through their allocation of resources to research and development. Once one allows for the inclusion of R and D in the production function, certain conceptual issues arise. First of all, one must specify how this input is to be measured. R and D input may be thought of as a stock variable, like capital. The investment in a research stock, therefore, yields returns, again much like capital investment, over a period of time. However, R and D is typically measured by flow variables: research spending as a ratio of some measure of industry size (e.g., sales or value-added) or the number of skilled personnel engaged in research as a ratio of total employment. This presents two important problems. First, there is generally a lag between research input and output. The effects of research effort on productivity may not manifest themselves until years after the research effort is expended (Scherer found an average lag between performed R and D and firm productivity of four to six years).[2] Second, the stock of R and D, like capital, may depreciate over time. The use of a flow research variable may be justified if the depreciation of R and D is minimal in any given time period and if annual flows do not vary much from year to year (there has been evidence that these flows have been fairly constant, at least at the two-digit industry level).[3] Another difficulty is that successful research may have impacts not only on measured output, but also on the quality of inputs; e.g., it can decrease the number of machine- or worker-hours needed in a production process. Usually, production functions have estimated the partial derivative of R and D with respect to output, but research quite often takes the form of output that is sold to other firms, or a new process that is used internally. Of course, in the case of research embodied in products sold to other firms, the productivity effects may not be "lost" but transferred to the receiving firms.

An intractable econometric problem is that the production function assumes that causality runs from research to output or productivity. Although these variables have been shown to be positively correlated, it is not clear that the direction of causality is strictly one-way. Increases in output and profits may induce firms to begin or expand their research programs.

The measurement of output in research-intensive industries is often made difficult by the introduction of new products. The structure of the innovating firm's industry, and the procedures of the statistical agencies that measure productivity indices, will determine how much of the improvement in product quality gets translated into productivity gains. The effect of the introduction of a new product, new photographic film, illustrates this point.[4] Suppose that the price and number of rolls of film sold by a firm are $1.00 and 8,000, respectively. Now, assume that the firm invents a better film (it can be developed in the camera, while the old type must be sent to a processor to be developed) that can be substituted for the old. The marginal and average cost of the new film both equal $1.00. Assume that if the price of the new film equals $2.00, all of the consumers of the old film will switch to the new film. The linear demand curve for the new film is given by the equation $Q = 10,100 - 100P$ and is shown in figure 4.

If the firm were able to operate as a monopoly, it would charge a profit-maximizing price of $51, where the marginal cost and the marginal revenue of the new film are equal at an output of 5,000 units. If 3,000 units of the old film were then sold at $1.00, the firm's revenue would rise from $8,000 to $255,000 while total costs would remain at $8,000. Measured productivity would in this case rise by a factor of almost 32.

Should the monopoly firm be able to engage in first degree price discrimination, the revenue it would receive would be higher still. Only under these circumstances would the firm appropriate the full value of the new product, i.e., by capturing the entire value of consumer surplus. The firm would charge the maximum price each consumer of the new film would pay. It would, therefore, sell 10,000 units of output and receive $510,000 ($\frac{1}{2}$ of AB $\times$ BC + $10,000). The average price charged would be $51. Revenue would have increased by a factor of 64, while total costs would have increased to only $10,000. Productivity in this case would rise by more than a factor of 51. If, on the other hand, the new film had been developed by the government and sold at marginal cost, the entire value of the improvement in product quality would be passed on to consumers. Since both the value of output and total cost would have increased in the same proportion, there would be no measured change in productivity. Between these two extremes of market structure are any number of intermediate cases and a number of possible values for measured productivity increases.

Statistical agencies must consider how product quality changes, such as the example presented here, will affect the construction of its price indices. A common practice is to leave the indices unchanged and to allow measured output to increase by the amount of additional revenue the firm receives subsequent to the introduction of the new product, and to measure the increase in costs by the additional value of resources used. Should the agency recognize the quality improvement (typically this is done after the product has been sold for some time), it may adjust its price index accordingly. For example, in the case of the new film, it may be determined that consumers are willing to pay at least twice as high a price as they paid for the old film. This can be interpreted as a halving of the real price. For the case where the firm sold 10,000 units of new film, the real output can be seen as having increased from 8,000 units to 20,000 units, while costs had increased from $8,000 to $10,000. The result is a doubling of measured productivity. As a practical matter, these types of adjustments are not often made.

Among the major CPI components only automobiles and, recently, housing prices are subject to quality adjustments. Lack of such quality adjustments can lead to very serious biases in some industries. In computers, for example, the national accounting convention has been to show no price change whatsoever. There is independent evidence, however, that the "real" price

Figure 4

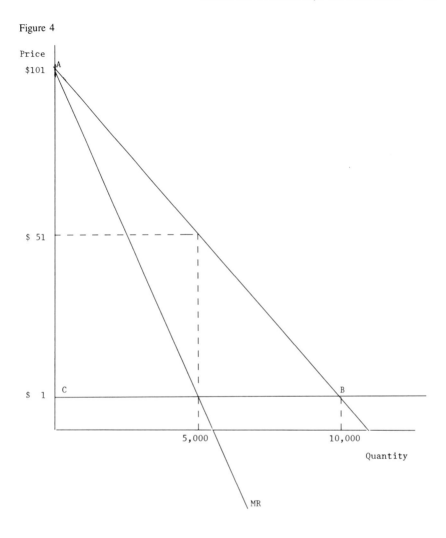

of computers has been falling by about 20 to 30 percent per year in the last decade, leading to a very serious downward bias in the estimate of output and productivity growth in this industry.[5]

To the extent that products like computers are used as inputs in other industries, these industries will have experienced increases in productivity that will compensate to some extent for the downward bias in the computer industries. This is due to the fact that the cost of purchasing the computers will understate the value of inputs. Therefore, the effect of the improvement in product quality may still show up (partially at least) in aggregate productivity, but not necessarily in the specific industry of origin.

Structure of the Productivity Model

Typical of the type of model used to estimate the effect of R and D on productivity is a simple Cobb-Douglas production function:

(1) $Q = e^{lt}R^aK^bL^cE$

where: Q = output in the ith industry in period t.

l = a parameter representing the influence of exogenous factors on output.

R, K = R and D, and plant and equipment stocks, respectively.

L = labor input.

E = an error term.

Since the productivity data that were used for the empirical analysis of this chapter were measured in terms of output per unit of labor, equation (1) can be divided on both sides by L; assuming that $b + c = 1$, and taking logarithms and differentiating with respect to time, equation (1) then becomes:

(2) $dLP = 1 + adR + bd(K/L) + lnE$

where: dLP = the percentage change in labor productivity.

$dR, d(K/L)$ = the percentage change in the stock of R and D and the capital-labor ratio, respectively.

Assuming that the depreciation of R and D is insignificant, Scherer has noted that the flow of R and D per unit of output, in a given time period, can be used to estimate the effect of research on productivity.[6] He estimated the parameters of a model similar to this for several time periods and several industry samples. To measure R and D he used two variables: 1974 research expenditures by industry of origin as a ratio of dollar output and R and D by industry of use (this variable was explained in chapter 3) per dollar of output. The latter variable was developed in an attempt to trace the effect of research performed in one industry on the industry (or industries) that ultimately used the new product or process that embodied the research effort. In theory, this variable should better explain the effect of research on productivity for those industries that are primarily technology "importers" than would their own R and D expenditures.[7]

Unfortunately, the R and D data used by Scherer were available for only one year (1974) because the Federal Trade Commission's Line of Business survey, from which the data were obtained, began with that year. This represents a potentially serious limitation given the lag between research effort and productivity (as mentioned previously). It is true that National Science Foundation data measuring research expenditures by manufacturing industries show a very high correlation over time (e.g., R and D/sales for 1973 and 1963 has a correlation of 0.98).[8] These data are at the two-digit level, however, and refer to research by industry of origin. Assuming that this stability holds at a more disaggregated level, and also for research by industry of use, the research data may be used in studies of productivity changes for earlier periods (what Scherer refers to as the "wrong lag" hypothesis.)[9]

In Scherer's regressions (for various time periods from 1964 to 1978) "used" R and D (RDU) was generally found to explain productivity growth better than "origin" R and D (RDO), but the results varied somewhat for different industry samples. He obtained three sets of estimates for industry labor productivity (one at the two-digit level and two mostly at the three-digit level). Given the tenuous nature of productivity estimates, it is important to note that any such data series must be interpreted carefully.

Griliches and Lichtenberg reexamined Scherer's results and used another set of data to perform similar statistical analyses.[10] Their dependent variable was a measure of the annual average growth in productivity. This variable was computed for two time periods (1964–1969 and 1973–1978) and was based on a four-digit measure of total factor productivity (for four inputs: capital, labor, energy, and materials) for 193 industries. Among their main findings was that, in spite of the difference in industry samples, "used" R and D had a greater impact on productivity growth than "origin" R and D, as Scherer had found. However, they also found that "origin" R and D also had a positive and statistically significant impact on productivity growth (although its influence was less than "used" R and D), a result that contrasted with most of the results obtained from Scherer's work.

The following section presents results from regressions similar to those run by Scherer, and Griliches and Lichtenberg, in that they are based on a productivity model that includes measures of "origin" and "used" R and D as explanatory variables. In addition, the regressions include measures of average industry concentration and the change in concentration. These variables are included in order to test the propositions of Demsetz and Peltzman. The goal is to see whether changes in productivity are affected by R and D while holding these concentration variables constant across industries and to observe whether there are differences in the regression results for increased and decreased concentration industries.

Empirical Results and Analysis

Data for the major part of the statistical analysis presented in this section were obtained for seventy-nine manufacturing industries for the 1963–1977 period. Table 21 shows the results of regressing the average annual growth of industry labor productivity (for 1963–1977 and 1967–1977) on several independent variables. GKL measures the average annual growth in industry capital-labor ratios. S63 and S67 represent the simple average four-firm, four-digit SIC concentration ratios for 1963–1977 and 1967–1977, respectively. ZIN63 is a bifurcated variable equal to the change in an industry's concentration ratio (1977 minus 1963) for industries that experienced increased, or no change in, concentration and is equal to zero otherwise. ZIN67 is similarly defined for 1967–1977. ZDE63 is equal to the change in concentration for industries that experienced decreased or no change in concentration for 1963–1977, and is equal to zero otherwise. ZDE67 is a similarly defined bifurcated variable for 1967–1977. RDO and RDU both represent industry research and development expenditures (for 1974) as ratios of 1972 industry constant dollar output.[11] Both research variables are based on Scherer's analysis of the Federal Trade Commission's Line of Business Survey. RDO refers to research spending by industry of origin, while RDU refers to research expenditures used by an industry through its "imports" from other industries.

Two separate time periods were selected in order to minimize the chance of selecting an initial year that had unusually low or high productivity. Both 1963 and 1967 were years of business cycle expansion, as was 1977. However, most of the 1970s were years of macroeconomic disruption and relatively low productivity growth. A priori, it was expected that this would probably cause the functional relationships that were estimated to be somewhat weaker in the shorter time period. In fact, this was found to have been the case. As noted in chapter 3, the industry sample has a high number of cases from the SIC 35 and 36 groups; therefore, it may be that the results that were obtained will not apply to a more random, or broader, range of industries. In spite of these and other potential limitations of the data set used, certain interesting results emerge from an analysis of table 21. It was surprising to see that GKL had so little explanatory power. One would have expected the sign for this variable to have been positive, but in each regression it has a negative sign and a very low t-statistic. The S63 and S67 variables, on the other hand, are positive and significant at the .01 level (using a one-tail test). The ZIN63 variable showed no evidence of a significant relationship with productivity in 1963–1977. In fact, rather than having the positive sign that is suggested by Peltzman's and Lustgarten's work, ZIN67 has a negative sign.

In order to compare the effects of the two research variables on productivity growth, separate regressions were run including either RDO or RDU. It is encouraging to find that the results for these variables conform to those obtained by Scherer and Griliches and Lichtenberg. That is, although RDO is positive and statistically

Table 21. Labor Productivity Regressions for U.S. Manufacturing Industries

Industry Sample		Independent Variables							R^2
1963–1977	Constant	GKL	S63	ZIN63	ZDE63	RDO	RDU		
(N = 77)	.012	-.028 (.35)	.014 (2.06)	.003 (.10)	-.067 (2.31)	.430 (2.85)	-----		.19
	.014	-.065 (.79)	.015 (2.16)	.013 (.45)	-.006 (2.28)	-----	.796 (3.01)		.20
1967–1977	Constant	GKL	S67	ZIN67	ZDE67	RDO	RDU		
(N = 79)	.016	-.047 (.53)	.022 (2.41)	-.068 (1.45)	-.002 (.06)	.172 (1.71)	-----		.13
	.015	-.069 (.78)	.023 (2.54)	-.057 (1.25)	-.019 (.53)	-----	.600 (1.84)		.14

Notes: The dependent variable is equal to the average annual growth of labor productivity for the indicated time period. GKL is the average annual growth of industry capital-labor ratios for either time period. S63 and S67 measure average four-firm, four-digit concentration ratios for 1963–1977 and 1967–1977, respectively. ZIN63 and ZIN67 equal the change in industry concentration ratios (1977 minus 1963 and 1977 minus 1967, respectively) for industries experiencing either increased or no change in concentration for the periods indicated, and are equal to zero otherwise. ZDE63 and ZDE67 are equal to the change in concentration for the same time periods for industries that experienced decreased or no change in concentration, and are equal to zero otherwise. RDO and RDU are ratios of 1974 research expenditures to 1972 constant dollar output by industry or origin and industry of use. T-statistics are in parentheses.

significant at the .01 level for 1963–1977, RDU has a much larger coefficient and has a greater t-value. As expected, the influence of both variables is not nearly so great for 1967–1977, but their relative influence is consistent with the other regression results.

Tables 22 and 23 show the results obtained when separate regressions were run for increased (IC) and decreased (DC) concentration industries (note: industries that experienced no change in concentration over either time period were included in both subsamples). For both subsamples of industries two separate regressions were run, each with either RDU or RDO as a measure of research intensity. Perhaps the most interesting result obtained from the regressions is that for IC industries RDO has greater explanatory power than RDU, while for the DC industries, the opposite is true: the coefficient of RDU is much higher than the coefficient of RDO (for both time periods) and has a greater t-value than RDO. In spite of the flaws in the data used, these results seem quite clear. The greater propensity for product innovation and product differentiation that was found among IC industries may help explain this result. It may also suggest that research spending by the largest firms in the IC industries is partly responsible for their ability to maintain or increase their market shares. The average concentration variable is positive in all four regressions in the two tables, but only in the IC regressions is it significant at at least the .10 level (using a one-tail test). The rate of labor productivity growth was greater among more concentrated industries in the IC sample. This result offers partial support for the Demsetz hypothesis that concentration and cost efficiency (to the extent that this is reflected by the growth of labor productivity) are positively related, especially among industries that have experienced increased concentration. However, the change in concentration variable in all but one regression is negative and is generally not statistically significant.

Tables 24 and 25 present some mean values for market structure variables associated with the industry samples. On average, there is little difference between IC and DC industries with respect to research intensity (RDU and RDO). DC industries had higher capital-labor ratios; this is consistent with the results presented in table 19. The variable PROC measures the percentage of industry patents that were directed toward process innovation.[12] The average values of PROC for DC industries are greater than the corresponding values for IC industries, although the difference is not very large for the 1967–1977 period (this may reflect that fact that changes in concentration for the 1963–1977 period reflect more fundamental forces and are less likely to be due to random influence).

The values of the PROC varies significantly across industries. Its average value for the thirty-seven SIC 35 and 36 industries was only 8.7, while the other forty-two industries had an average value of 38.2. This reflects the fact that the SIC 35 and 36 industries produce machinery and other inputs that are sold to other firms. Apparently, very few of their own patented research efforts are directed toward internal processes. PROC is positively correlated with average concentra-

Table 22. Labor Productivity Regressions for Increased Concentration and Decreased Concentration Industries (1963–1977)

Industry Sample	Constant	Independent Variables						R^2
		GKL	S63	Z63	RDO	RDU		
Increased Concentration (N = 35)	.011	.034 (.25)	.017 (1.55)	.00 (.14)	-----	.634 (.86)		.12
	.009	.029 (.23)	.018 (1.80)	-.002 (.05)	.489 (2.19)	-----		.22
Decreased Concentration (N = 53)	.019	-.139 (1.44)	.012 (1.49)	-.057 (1.96)	-----	.847 (3.25)		.24
	.017	-.086 (.87)	.010 (1.29)	-.055 (1.84)	.396 (2.19)	-----		.16

Notes: Variable definitions are given in table 21. T-statistics are in parentheses.

Table 23. Labor Productivity Regressions for Increased Concentration and Decreased Concentration Industries (1967–1977)

Industry Sample	Independent Variables						R^2
	Constant	GKL	G67	Z67	RDO	RDU	
Increased Concentration (N = 31)	.006	.028 (.20)	.031 (2.23)	-.055 (.02)	-----	.924 (1.00)	.23
	.004	-.018 (.56)	.032 (2.54)	-.055 (1.13)	.651 (2.45)	-----	.35
Decreased Concentration (N = 52)	.020	-.137 (1.20)	.016 (1.30)	-.028 (.71)	-----	.583 (1.63)	.11
	.021	-.108 (.94)	.015 (1.21)	-.017 (.38)	.115 (1.02)	-----	.08

Notes: Variable definitions are given in table 21. T-statistics are in parentheses.

Table 24. Mean Values of Market Structure Variables (1963-1977)

Industry Sample	Variables							
	CR77	CR63	KL76	RDU	RDO	PROC	LP
All Industries (N = 79)	44.5 (20.8)	45.9 (21.1)	15.2 (12.1)	.003 (.006)	.008 (.019)	24.4 (29.6)	.024 (.017)
Increased Concentration Industries (N = 35)	46.6 (21.6)	41.1 (20.7)	14.7 (12.1)	.002 (.003)	.007 (.009)	19.8 (29.3)	.021 (.013)
Decreased Concentration Industries (N = 53)	41.0 (19.9)	47.7 (20.5)	16.3 (13.7)	.002 (.006)	.006 (.009)	27.1 (30.8)	.025 .012

Notes: CR77 and CR63 refer to industry concentration ratios for 1977 and 1963, respectively. KL76 is the industry capital-labor ratio for 1976. PROC is the percentage of industry patents that are directed toward process innovation. LP is the average annual growth of labor productivity. RDU and RDO are defined in table 21. Figures in parentheses are standard deviations.

Table 25. Mean Values of Market Structure Variables (1967–1977)

Industry Sample	Variables							
	CR77	CR63	KL76	RDU	RDO	PROC	LP	
All Industries (N = 79)	44.5 (20.8)	46.1 (20.3)	15.2 (12.1)	.003 (.006)	.008 (.019)	24.4 (29.6)	.024 (.017)	
Increased Concentration Industries (N = 35)	51.8 (20.8)	46.0 (20.3)	14.0 (8.9)	.002 (.003)	.008 (.010)	23.3 (30.1)	.021 (.015)	
Decreased Concentration Industries (N = 52)	40.0 (19.3)	45.8 (20.2)	15.7 (13.3)	.003 (.007)	.008 (.022)	25.2 (30.9)	.025 (.017)	

Notes: Variable definitions are given in table 24.

tions; the simple correlations of PROC with S67 and S63 for all industries are .30 and .32, respectively. This is suggestive of Comanor's observation of a high correlation between research intensity and concentration among those industries that have a low propensity for product differentiation. Finally, one may note that the growth of labor productivity was somewhat greater for the DC industries in both time periods.[13]

The possible flaws associated with the data used for this study have already been mentioned. As a partial check on the validity of the generalizations made in this section, another data set was obtained for fifty-one four-digit SIC industries.[14] Although not enough observations were obtained to compare separate regression results for DC and IC industries, descriptive statistics for these industry groups (for the period 1963–1977) were obtained and are presented in table 26. the most dramatic results shown in the table were the very high positive correlation between labor productivity growth and change in concentration relationship for the IC industries (.63), while the corresponding relationship for the DC industries was very close to zero (.01). There was also a higher positive correlation between average concentration and productivity growth among the IC industries than the DC industries. These results lend support to the Demsetz hypothesis that associates increased concentration with reductions in average costs of production. One possible explanation for these findings is the lower values of CR77 and CR63 for IC industries shown in table 26 relative to the corresponding values found in table 24. This could indicate significant scale economies associated with increased concentration among the IC industries in the second sample. However, the weaker correlations shown between productivity and both RDO and RDU emphasize the tentative nature of results based on limited sample sizes.

Summary and Conclusions

Previous analyses of the relationship between market structure and research intensity have found little support for the simple Schumpeterian hypothesis that monopoly power is necessary for successful innovation or that industry R and D activity increases monotonically with firm size or industrial concentration. The evidence presented in preceding chapters has also failed to support this hypothesis. Tables 6 and 7 from chapter 3 presented correlations between two measures of research intensity (R and D spending ratios by industry of use, or RDU, and by industry of origin, or RDO) and several variables. For the seventy-nine industries for which data were obtained, there was little evidence of a positive relationship between either R and D measure and four-firm concentration ratios for 1977 or 1963. In fact, for some subgroups of industries the correlation was negative. Similarly, changes in industry concentration showed no systematic correlation with research intensity, except for the group of industries that were classified as the most research-intensive. For this latter group, there was a positive relationship

Table 26.   Descriptive Statistics for 51 Four-Digit SIC Industries
(1963–1977)

Increased Concentration Industries (N = 31)

Correlation of dLP with:				
Z63	S63	RDO	RDU	PROC
.63	.22	.14	.02	.05

	Industry Mean and Standard Deviation Values				
	dLP	CR77	CR63	RDO	RDU	PROC
Mean	.023	42.8	36.5	.014	.008	39.3
Standard Deviation	.012	24.2	22.9	.015	.007	37.1

Decreased Concentration Industries (N = 23)

Correlation of dLP with:				
Z63	S63	RDO	RDU	PROC
.01	.06	-.04	.01	.19

	Industry Mean and Standard Deviation Values				
	dLP	CR77	CR63	RDO	RDU	PROC
Mean	.027	41.5	46.7	.013	.010	31.4
Standard Deviation	.014	21.3	22.9	.019	.018	24.8

between RDO and change in concentration. There were very strong, positive correlations between research intensity and both market growth and the growth of labor productivity. However, these correlations were different for the research-intensive and other industry groups. In particular, there was strong evidence that RDU was positively related to productivity growth for the non-research-intensive industries, but there was a very low correlation between RDO and market growth for these same industries. On the other hand, RDO has a positive correlation with productivity growth for the research-intensive industries, a result that accords with a priori expectations. In spite of the crudeness of the data used for these tables, the differences in the relationships shown for RDU and RDO emphasize the hazards of attributing the effects of research and technological change solely to the industries of origin.

Several economists have interpreted changes in concentration, along with the level of industry concentration, as reflections of differences in the costs of production of firms in these industries. Therefore, studies that use collusion to explain the often found positive correlation between concentration and profits across U.S. industries may be in error. There has been some empirical support for this differential cost efficiency hypothesis, but the source (or sources) of the cost efficiencies have been subject to some differences of opinion. Should large firms in high, or increasing, concentration industries be more efficient than other firms in these same industries, one may attribute this difference to economies of scale, superior management, or, as Peltzman suggests, cost-reducing technological innovation undertaken by the large firms. Should Peltzman's interpretation be correct, one would expect that research expenditures, especially for process innovation, would be an important catalyst for this type of innovation. However, Peltzman did not use R and D as an explanatory variable in his empirical tests. In fact, in chapter 4's profile of industries that had experienced changes in concentration in the past, consumer goods industries had a higher representation among increased concentration industries, and producer goods industries were more common among decreased concentration industries. In addition, DC industries had, on average, higher capital-labor ratios, market sizes, wages paid, and research intensity. It appears plausible to assume that product innovation and product differentiation were more common among IC industries than among DC industries. The ability of large firms in IC industries successfully to introduce new products (which may, as Scherer explained, be followed by significant reductions in production costs) may explain their increases in market shares. There is some evidence to indicate that the appropriability of process innovation is less than the appropriability of product innovation. The greater propensity for process innovation among firms in DC industries may be partly responsible for the loss of market share of large firms.

The regression results of this chapter showed that higher levels of concentration are associated with higher rates of productivity growth; there is some indication that this effect is stronger for IC industries. The change in concentration variable, however, has a negligible impact on productivity growth for IC industries; there is a negative relationship for DC industries, although this varies considerably between time periods. There is no indication that reductions in concentration are associated with cost increases.

There is a clear difference for the seventy-nine industry sample with respect to the effects of RDO and RDU on productivity growth for IC and DC industries. "Imported" research has a stronger effect on productivity growth for DC industries (and, in fact, may be one reason for the decline in concentration). Although RDO is positively significant for both DC and IC regressions, the effect in the latter regressions is stronger, providing support for the view that research in these industries is more oriented toward product innovation and differentiation (the values for PROC are also consistent with this interpretation). If large firms in IC industries use product differentiation to enhance appropriability, then with this would come the ability to extract greater returns from research investments. In other words, successful product innovation would enable the innovating firms to charge a price that reflected some part of the value of the new product. In fact, this may also be one reason for the positive coefficient for the average concentration variable, since large firms in high concentration industries would have greater control over price than firms in low concentration industries.

The statistical analysis of the fifty-one industry sample summarized in table 26 produced some results that differed from those obtained with the larger sample. For the IC industries, there was a positive correlation between average concentration and productivity growth, and RDO had a higher positive correlation with productivity growth than did RDU. The correlations for DC industries were uniformly low. By far the most significant relationship, however, was the positive correlation between productivity growth and change in concentration for IC industries. Undoubtedly, the effect of changes in concentration on productivity growth varies a great deal for different groups of industries. The average levels of concentration for the IC industries included in the fifty-one industry sample (shown in table 26) are lower than the corresponding values for IC industries in the larger sample (table 24). This may suggest that significant economies of scale were achieved by growing firms in the former sample.

The results that were obtained here are interesting in themselves, but also highlight the need for more accurate, comprehensive data for productivity growth and research intensity. For example, it would be useful to have access to data that allowed for the examination of the effects of research and concentration on industries within the same two-digit SIC classifications. It is likely that these effects would be different across these industry categories. Given the difficulties associated with measuring the productivity effects of industries that experience technological change, it would be inappropriate to make quantitative generalizations concerning the statistical results shown in this chapter. However, some of the qualitative results that were obtained are worthy of emphasis. As was indicated above, these included the differential effects of RDO and RDU for IC and DC industries. In addition, little evidence was found of the cost-increasing effects of decreased concentration that were found by Lustgarten. There was some support for Demsetz' hypothesis that predicts greater cost efficiency or productivity growth for high-concentration industries than for low-concentration industries. It seems unlikely, however, that these efficiencies can be ascribed to the cost-reducing technological innovation that Peltzman associated with increased concentration.

Appendix

Sources of Data

The data used in the empirical analyses of this work were taken from a number of sources. The four-firm, four-digit SIC concentration ratios (based on industry sales) were taken from the *Census of Manufacturers* for 1972 and 1977. The market growth variables shown in tables 6 and 7 are equal to the average annual growth rates of constant dollar output (in millions of 1972 dollars) between 1963 and 1976 (G63) and between 1967 and 1976 (G67). These growth rates were estimated with the use of natural logs. The growth of labor productivity variables (PROD63 and PROD67 in tables 6 and 7; the dependent variables of the regression results shown in tables 21, 22, and 23; LP in tables 24 and 25) were computed in a similar manner for the periods 1963–1967 and 1967–1976, using a measure of constant dollar output per-worker-hour. Both of these variables were taken from Bureau of Labor Statistics Bulletin 2018, "Time Series Data for Input-Output Industries" (data were not available for 1977). The data were generally at the three-digit level.

The data from table 19 include four-digit capital-labor ratios taken from *Industry Profiles, 1958–1968*, which are equal to the value of capital divided by total employment. The wage variable (wages per-worker per-man-hour) and industry value-added are both four-digit variables taken from the *Census of Manufacturers*. The research data are for two-digit industries taken from *Research and Development in Industry 1973* (published by the National Science Foundation). Four-digit data for the percentage of output sold to consumers (for 1963) were taken from a U.S. Department of Commerce publication, *Input-Output Structure of the U.S. Economy: 1963*.

Tables 21 through 26 refer to several other variables in addition to those already mentioned. GKL and KL76 were compiled using values for net industry capital stock in millions of constant (1972) dollars at the three-digit level. Computer print-outs of this information were provided by the Office of Economic Growth of the Bureau of Labor Statistics for the years 1958 to 1976. These figures were then divided by total employment (all workers, in thousands, taken from "Time Series Data for Input-Output Industries") to obtain capital-labor ratios, and the annual (log) change in these ratios. RDO and RDU are four-digit data taken from Scherer's "Using Linked Patent and R&D Data to Measure Interindustry Technology Flows." This is also the source for the four-digit PROC variable referred to in tables 24, 25, and 26.

The seventy-nine-industry sample represented a combination of data from various sources. This introduces certain biases since, e.g., three-digit productivity data had to be used with four-digit concentration and research data. Productivity growth rates for three-digit industries, then, were used to estimate growth rates for four-digit industries. The four-digit productivity data obtained for the fifty-one-industry sample (shown in table 26) are from "Productivity Measures for Selected Industries, 1954–81," Bureau of Labor Statistics Bulletin 2155.

Notes

Chapter 1

1. Robert Solow, "Technical Change and the Aggregate Production Function," *Review of Economics and Statistics* 39 (August 1957): 312-20.

2. W. Gruber, D. Mehta and R. Vernon, "The R and D Factor in International Trade and International Investment," *Journal of Political Economy* 75 (February 1976): 28.

3. Wassily Leontief, "Domestic Production and Foreign Trade, the American Capital Position Re-examined," in *AEA Readings in International Economics,* ed. Ronald Jones and Harry Johnson (Homewood, Ill.: Richard D. Irwin, 1968): 503-27.

4. Morton I. Kamien and Nancy L. Schwartz, "Market Structure and Innovation: A Survey," *Journal of Economic Literature* 13 (March 1975): 1.

5. Ibid., 11.

6. See, for example, Edwin Mansfield, *Industrial Research and Technological Innovation: An Econometric Analysis* (New York: W.W. Norton and Co., 1968).

7. Stephen Magee, "Multinational Corporations, the Industry Technology Cycle and Development," *Journal of World Trade Law* 2 (July/August 1977): 297.

8. Edwin Mansfield, "Technology and Technological Change," in *Economic Analysis and the Multinational Enterprise,* ed. John H. Dunning (New York: Praeger, 1974).

9. James Cook, "A Game Any Number Can Play," *Forbes* 123 (June 1979): 56-62.

10. Ibid., 50.

11. E. Mansfield, A. Romeo and S. Wagner, "Foreign Trade and U.S. Research and Development," *Review of Economics and Statistics* 61 (February 1979): 49-57.

12. Arthur M. Louis, "SmithKline Finds Rich Is Better," *Fortune* 102 (June 1980): 62-66.

13. Ibid., 65.

14. Stephen Hymer, *The International Operations of National Firms: A Study of Direct Foreign Investment* (Cambridge: MIT Press, 1976); Richard Caves, "International Corporations: The Industrial Economics of Foreign Investment," *Economica* 38 (February 1971): 1-27.

15. Raymond Vernon, *Storm Over the Multinationals* (Cambridge: Harvard University Press, 1977): 66-67.

16. Leonard Weiss, "The Concentration-Profits Relationship and Antitrust," in *Industrial Concentration: The New Learning,* ed. H. Goldschmid, H. Mann and J. Weston (Boston: Little, Brown and Co., 1974): 184–223.

17. Yale Brozen, "Bain's Concentration and Rates of Return Revisited," *Journal of Law and Economics* 14 (October 1971): 351–69.

18. Harold Demsetz, "Industry Structure, Market Rivalry and Public Policy," *Journal of Law and Economics* 16 (April 1973): 1–9.

19. Sam Peltzman, "The Gains and Losses From Industrial Concentration," *Journal of Law and Economics* 20 (October 1977): 229–63.

20. Steven Lustgarten, "Gains and Losses From Industrial Concentration," *Journal of Law and Economics* 22 (April 1979): 183–90.

21. Frederic M. Scherer, "The Causes and Consequences of Rising Industrial Concentration," *Journal of Law and Economics* 22 (April 1979): 191–208.

Chapter 2

1. Leontief, "Domestic Production," 503–27. An early criticism of Hecksher-Ohlin was given by John Williams, "The Theory of International Trade Reconsidered," *Economic Journal* 39 (June 1929): 195–209. A particularly insightful criticism of the theory was given by Romney Robinson, "Factor Proportions and Comparative Advantage," in *AEA Readings in International Economics,* ed. Jones and Johnson, 3–23.

2. See, for example, Gary Hufbauer, "The Impact of National Characteristics and Technology on the Commodity Composition of Trade in Manufactured Goods," in *The Technology Factor in International Trade,* ed. Raymond Vernon (New York: National Bureau of Economic Research, 1970), 145–231.

3. Raymond Vernon, "International Investment and International Trade in the Product Cycle," *Quarterly Journal of Economics* 80 (May 1966): 190.

4. Among the best known of these studies are: John Diebold, "Is the Gap Technological?" *Foreign Affairs* 46 (January 1968): 276–91. Donald Keesing, "Labor Skills and Comparative Advantage," *American Economic Review* (p) 56 (May 1966): 249–58, and "The Impact of R and D on United States Trade," *Journal of Political Economy* 75 (February 1967): 34–48. Irving Kravis, "Availability and Other Influences on the Commodity Composition of Trade," *Journal of Political Economy* 64 (April 1956): 287–94, and "Wages and Foreign Trade," *Review of Economics and Statistics* 38 (August 1956): 14–38.

5. Gruber, Mehta and Vernon, "The R and D Factor," 20–37.

6. William Gruber and Raymond Vernon, "The Technology Factor in the World Trade Matrix," in *The Technology Factor,* 233–72.

7. Mansfield, Romeo and Wagner, "Foreign Trade," 49–57.

8. Caves, "International Corporations," 1–27.

9. Small firms have developed many successful inventions. See Stephen Magee, "Multinational Corporations," 300–301.

10. Mansfield, "Technology and Technological Change," in *Economic Analysis.*

11. Michael Waldholz, "Marketing Often is the Key to Success of Prescription Drugs," *The Wall Street Journal,* Dec. 28, 1981.

12. Vernon, *Storm*, 48–49.

13. Edwin Mansfield, *Industrial Research*, 16.

14. See Harry Johnson, "The Efficiency and Welfare Implications of the International Corporation," in *The International Corporation*, ed. Charles Kindleberger (Boston: MIT Press, 1970), 39–40.

15. Nathan Rosenberg, *Perspectives on Technology* (New York: Cambridge University Press, 1976).

16. George Stigler, "The Division of Labor is Limited by the Extent of the Market," *Journal of Political Economy* 59 (June 1951): 185–93.

17. Rosenberg, *Perspectives*, 141–44.

18. Jack Baranson, "Is There a Direct Route to Development?" *Challenge* 12 (July 1964): 33.

19. Vernon, "Product Cycle," 190–207.

20. Ibid., 198–99.

21. Note that this technology need not be new; e.g., the technology to produce synthetic fuels and electric automobiles has been available for decades. Commercial application of these technologies will probably not begin on a large scale until at least the 1990s.

22. Total sales by majority-owned foreign affiliates of U.S. companies in all countries were over $500 billion in 1976. William Chung, "Sales of Majority-Owned Foreign Affiliates of U.S. Companies, 1976," *Survey of Current Business* 58 (March 1978): 31–40.

23. Vernon, "Product Cycle," 201–2.

24. Harry Johnson, "Aspects of Patents and Licenses as Stimuli to Innovation." *Weltwirtschaftliches Archiv* 112 (1973): 420–21.

25. Magee, "Multinational Corporations," 297.

26. Edwin Mansfield, *The Economics of Technological Change* (New York: W.W. Norton and Co., 1968), 47.

27. Magee, "Multinational Corporations," 301.

28. Richard Nelson, "Introduction," in *The Rate and Direction of Inventive Activity*, ed. Richard Nelson (Princeton: Princeton University Press, 1962), 3–16.

29. Stephen Magee, "Multinational Corporations," 306.

30. Once a new product is marketed, even with patent protection, emulating firms are not prohibited from producing a similar product. Patented inventions have been shown to be often imitated within a few years of their introduction. Since ideas and inventions are developed and sold in the first stage, property rights are better defined here than in the innovation stage.

Chapter 3

1. William Davidson, "Patterns of Factor-Saving Innovation in the Industrialized World," *European Economic Review* 8 (October 1976): 207–17.

2. Louis Wells, "A Product Life Cycle for International Trade?" *Journal of Marketing* 32 (July 1968): 1–6.

3. The traditional presentation of the Hecksher-Ohlin factor proportions theory of trade assumes that capital and labor are the two factors of production used by producers in two trading coun-

tries. However, one may alternatively distinguish human and non-human capital, or skilled and unskilled labor. Leontief's paradox may be resolved within the factor proportions framework if one considers the United States to have had a comparative advantage in the production of goods that require relatively large amounts of skilled labor, or human capital. Studies have also shown that the industries that Leontief found to be heavy importers, imported products that had a high natural resource content. The capital intensity found in these industries, then, may have masked high resource requirements and a complementarity between capital and natural resources in production. See Peter H. Lindert and Charles Kindleberger, *International Economics,* 7th ed. (Homewood, Ill.: Richard D. Irwin, 1982): 68–73.

4. Darius Gaskins, "Dynamic Limit Pricing Model: Optimal Pricing Under the Threat of Entry," *Journal of Economic Theory* 3 (September 1971): 306–22.

5. Stephen Magee, "Application of the Dynamic Limit Pricing Model to the Price of Technology and International Technology Transfer," in *Optimal Policies, Control Theory and Technology Exports* (New York: North-Holland Publishing Co., 1977), 203–23.

6. Stephen Magee, "Information and the Multinational Corporation: An Appropriability Theory of Direct Foreign Investment," in *The New International Economic Order: The North-South Debate,* ed. Jagdish Bhagwati (Cambridge: MIT Press, 1977), 322.

7. Ibid., 331.

8. Ibid. The youngest industry was 11.7 years old while 39.3 years was the age of the oldest industry. Magee then selected the midpoint of the range of these numbers, or 25.5 years.

9. Gaskins, "Dynamic Limit Pricing Model," 320.

10. Stephen Magee, "Multinational Corporations," 297.

11. Ibid., 298.

12. Hufbauer, "The Impact of National Characteristics," in *The Technology Factor,* 145–231.

13. Ibid., 188.

14. Richard Nelson and Sidney Winter, "The Schumpeterian Tradeoff Revisited," *American Economic Review* 72 (March 1982): 114–32.

15. Edwin Mansfield, "Technological Change and Market Structure," *American Economic Review* (p) 73 (May 1983): 205–9.

16. Ibid., 207.

17. Ibid., 208.

18. Frederic M. Scherer, "Inter-industry Technology Flows and Productivity Growth," *Review of Economics and Statistics* 64 (November 1982): 627.

19. A comprehensive critique of the reliability of the line of business data used in several studies, including Scherer's, is given by: George J. Benston, "The Validity of Profits-Structure Studies with Particular Reference to the FTC's Line of Business Data," *American Economic Review* 75 (March 1985): 37–67.

20. Descriptions of the data used are found in the appendix on p. 87.

21. Scherer, "Inter-industry Technology Flows," 629.

22. It could be hypothesized that high concentration industries in years prior to 1974 were prone to develop research programs and that 1977 concentration ratios are inappropriate to use for the correlations presented. In any event, the choice of year appears to be unimportant.

23. See, for example, the comments of John Stopford and Louis Wells, *Managing the Multinational Enterprise* (New York: Basic Books, 1972), 130.

24. Stopford and Wells, *Managing,* 132–42.

25. J. Behrman and W. Schmidt, "New Data on Foreign Licensing," *Patent, Trademark, Copyright Journal of Research and Education* (Winter 1959): 357–88.

26. Ibid., 381–82.

27. National Industrial Conference Board, *Appraising Foreign Licensing Performance* (New York: National Industrial Conference Board, 1969).

28. Mansfield, Romeo and Wagner, "Foreign Trade," 49–57.

29. Ibid., 55.

30. E. Mansfield, A. Romeo, M. Schwartz, D. Teece, S. Wagner and P. Brach. *Technology Transfer, Productivity, and Economic Policy* (New York: W. W. Norton & Co., 1982), 211.

31. Ibid., 48.

32. Vernon, "Product Cycle," 201–2.

33. Vernon, *Storm,* 66–67.

34. Paul Strassman, *Technological Change and Economic Development* (Ithaca, New York: Cornell University Press, 1968), 25–27.

35. David Teece, *The Multinational Corporation and the Resource Cost of International Technology Transfer* (Cambridge: Ballinger Publishing, 1976).

36. Joseph Schumpeter, *Capitalism, Socialism, and Democracy,* 3rd ed. (New York: Harper, 1950), 106.

37. Maria Shao, "Exxon's Mining Unit Finds It Tough Going After 16 Years in Field," *The Wall Street Journal,* August 31, 1982.

38. Ibid.

39. Frederic M. Scherer, *Industrial Market Structure and Economic Performance* (Chicago: Rand McNally, 1970), 354.

40. James Worley, "Industrial Research and the New Competition," *Journal of Political Economy* 69 (April 1961): 183–86.

41. William Comanor, "Market Research, Product Differentiation, and Industrial Research," *Quarterly Journal of Economics* 81 (November 1967): 641.

42. Edwin Mansfield, "Industrial Research and Development Expenditures: Determinants, Prospects, and Relation to Size of Firm and Inventive Output," *Journal of Political Economy* 72 (August 1964): 337.

43. Scherer, *Industrial Market Structure,* 360–61.

44. Jesse Markham, "Market Structure, Business Conduct, and Innovation," *American Economic Review* (p) 55 (May 1965): 323–32; Scherer, *Industrial Market Strucutre,* 361.

45. Comanor, "Market Research."

46. Edwin Mansfield, "Composition of R and D Expenditures: Relationship to Size of Firm, Concentration, and Innovative Output," *Review of Economics and Statistics* 63 (November 1981): 610–15.

Chapter 4

1.   Weiss, "The Concentration-Profits Relationship," in *Industrial Concentration,* 202.

2.   Joseph Bain, "Relation of Profit Rate to Industry Concentration," *Quarterly Journal of Economics* 65 (August 1951): 293–324.

3.   Brozen, "Bain's Concentration," 351–69.

4.   Demsetz, "Industry Structure," 1–9.

5.   Ibid., 7.

6.   Ibid., 8.

7.   Ronald Bond and Warren Greenberg, "Industry Structure, Market Rivalry and Public Policy: A Comment," *Journal of Law and Economics* 19 (April 1976): 203.

8.   Harold Demsetz, "More on Collusion and Advertising: A Reply," *Journal of Law and Economics* 19 (April 1976): 206–7.

9.   Harold Demsetz, *The Market Concentration Doctrine* (Washington: American Enterprise Institute, 1973), 24.

10. Demsetz, "Industry Structure, Market Rivalry," 8.

11. Peltzman, "The Gains and Losses," 231–32.

12. Ibid., 240–41.

13. Ibid., 243.

14. Capital costs for both years were unavailable. Peltzman assumed that each industry's capital costs were proportional to the gross book value of plant and equipment, for which data could be obtained.

15. Peltzman, "The Gains and Losses," 244.

16. Note that Peltzman included industries whose concentration had not changed in both subsamples.

17. Peltzman, "The Gains and Losses," 250.

18. Ibid., 252.

19. Ibid., 230–33.

20. Ibid., 233.

21. Ibid., 235.

22. Ibid., 262.

23. Nelson and Winter, "The Schumpeterian Tradeoff," 116–17.

24. Ibid., 116.

25. Ibid., 117.

26. Overall, about three-fourths of privately financed R and D is spent on product development. Scherer, "Inter-industry Technology Flows," 629.

27. Peltzman, "The Gains and Losses," 243.

28. Scherer, "The Causes and Consequences," 191–208.

29. Ibid., 193.

30. Ibid., 192.

31. The four-digit SIC production indexes were taken from the *Census of Manufacturers, 1972.* Explanation of the other data used is found in the appendix on p. 87.

32. Scherer, "The Causes and Consequences," 192.

33. Ibid.

34. Comanor, "Market Research," 651.

35. Alternatively, one would expect to find that research spending for process innovation would be greater among IC industries. Although the research data in table 19 do not distinguish spending for process and product innovation, the consumer goods orientation of the IC industries suggests that process innovation would not be more common than among DC industries.

36. Lustgarten, "Gains and Losses," 183–90.

37. Ibid., 183–86.

38. Ibid., 186.

39. Ibid., 190.

40. Scherer, "The Causes and Consequences," 200.

41. Ibid., 205.

42. Sam Peltzman, "The Causes and Consequences of Rising Industrial Concentration: A Reply," *Journal of Law and Economics* 22 (April 1979): 209.

43. The experience curve, or learning curve phenomenon, had been observed years before it was used as a tool by management consultants. For example, "The Horndal iron works in Sweden had no new investment . . . for a period of 15 years, yet productivity . . . rose . . . 2% per annum . . . which can only be [ascribed] to learning from experience." Kenneth Arrow, "The Economic Implications of Learning by Doing," *Review of Economic Studies* 29 (June 1962): 155–73.

44. Walter Kiechel, "The Decline of the Experience Curve," *Fortune* 104 (October 1981): 139–46.

45. John McGee, "Efficiency and Economies of Size," in *Industrial Concentration,* 64.

46. Thomas J. Peters and Robert H. Waterman, Jr., *In Search of Excellence* (New York: Harper & Row, 1982).

47. Ibid., 272–73, 275.

48. Edwin Mansfield, "Size of Firm, Market Structure, and Innovation," in *In Defense of Industrial Concentration* (New York: Praeger Publishers, 1971): 111.

49. Ibid., 111–12.

50. W.E.G. Salter, *Productivity and Technical Change* (Cambridge: Cambridge University Press, 1960).

Chapter 5

1. Zvi Griliches, "Issues in Assessing the Contribution of Research and Development to Productivity Growth," *Bell Journal of Economics* 71 (May 1981): 92–116.

2. Scherer, "Inter-industry Technology Flows," 629.

3. Ibid.

4. This example was used by Griliches, "Issues in Assessing," 98–99.

5. Ibid., 99.

6. Scherer, "Inter-industry Technology," 628.

7. Frederic M. Scherer, "Using Linked Patent and R & D Data to Measure Inter-industry Technology Flows," in *R & D, Patents and Productivity*, ed. Zvi Griliches (Chicago: University of Chicago Press, 1984), 417–64. In this work Scherer explains the process by which he computed his "used" R and D variable in considerable detail (see also Mansfield's comments, following Scherer's exposition, for a critique of his techniques). Scherer estimated the flow of research to industries of use from industries of origin through the vehicle of patents. A sample of over 15,000 patents was examined in order to ascertain those industries that would most likely use the inventions. "Each patent then became, in effect, a carrier of the average R & D expenditure per patent in its origin [line of business], transmitting by a fairly complicated algorithm those expenditures out to the coded, using industries." Ibid., 423.

8. Scherer, "Inter-industry Technology Flows," 629.

9. Zvi Griliches and Frank Lichtenberg, "Interindustry Technology Flows and Productivity Growth: A Reexamination," *Review of Economics and Statistics* 66 (May 1984): 327. Griliches and Lichtenberg reported evidence of stable R and D expenditures over time at a more disaggregated level.

10. Ibid. Scherer's combined industry process R and D with R and D embodied in purchases of inputs in some of his regressions. Griliches and Lichtenberg separated these two research values and discovered that the explanatory power of "used" R and D appeared to be due primarily to the own-process component.

11. The research variables were taken from Scherer, "Using Linked Patent," 450–59.

12. Ibid.

13. Allen found no significant differences in productivity growth rates of nineteen industries that were classified as "highly concentrated" (i.e., with declining or stable concentration from 1939 to 1964) or "low concentration" (for industries with a four-firm concentration ratio less than 50). B.T. Allen, "Concentration and Economic Progress: Note," *American Economic Review* 59 (September 1969): 600–604.

14. These data are described in the appendix on p. 87.

Bibliography

Allen, B. "Concentration and Economic Progress: Note." *American Economic Review* 59 (September 1969): 600–604.

Arrow, K. "The Economic Implications of Learning by Doing." *Review of Economic Studies* 29 (June 1962): 155–73.

Bain, J. "Relation of Profit Rate to Industry Concentration." *Quarterly Journal of Economics* 65 (August 1951): 293–324.

Baranson, J. "Is There a Direct Route to Development?" *Challenge* 12 (July 1964): 32–35.

Behrman, J. and Schmidt, W. "New Data on Foreign Licensing." *Patent, Trademark, Copyright Journal of Research and Education* (Winter 1959): 357–88.

Benston, "The Validity of Profits-Structure with Particular Reference to the FTC's Line of Business Data." *American Economic Review* 75 (March 1985): 36–67.

Bond, R. and Greenberg, W. "Industry Structure, Market Rivalry, and Public Policy: A Comment." *Journal of Law and Economics* 19 (April 1976): 201–4.

Brozen, Y. "Bain's Concentration and Rates of Return Revisited." *Journal of Law and Economics* 14 (October 1971): 351–69.

Caves, R. "International Corporations: The Industrial Economics of Foreign Investment." *Economics* 38 (February 1971): 1–27.

Chung, W. "Sales of Majority-Owned Foreign Affiliates of U.S. Companies, 1976." *Survey of Current Business* 58 (March 1978): 31–40.

Comanor, W. "Market Research, Product Differentiation, and Industrial Research." *Quarterly Journal of Economics* 81 (November 1967): 639–57.

Cook, J. "A Game Any Number Can Play." *Forbes* 123 (June 1979): 49–60.

Davidson, W. "Patterns of Factor-Saving Innovation in the Industrialized World." *European Economic Review* 8 (October 1976): 207–17.

Demsetz, H. "More on Collusion and Advertising: A Reply." *Journal of Law and Economics* 19 (April 1976): 205–9.

_____. *The Market Concentration Doctrine*. Washington: American Enterprise Institute, 1973.

_____. "Industry Structure, Market Rivalry, and Public Policy." *Journal of Law and Economics* 16 (April 1973): 1–9.

Denison, E. *The Sources of Growth in the United States and the Alternatives Before Us*. New York: Committee for Economic Development, 1962.

Diebold, J. "Is the Gap Technological?" *Foreign Affairs* 46 (January 1968): 276–91.

Dunning, J., ed. *Economic Analysis and the Multinational Enterprise*. New York: Praeger, 1974.

Gaskins, D. "Dynamic Limit Pricing: Optimal Pricing Under the Threat of Entry." *Journal of Economic Theory* 3 (September 1971): 306–22.

Goldschmid, H., Mann, H., and Weston, J., eds. *Industrial Concentration: The New Learning*. New York: Holt, Rinehart and Winston, 1971.

Griliches, Z. "Issues in Assessing the Contribution of Research and Development to Productivity Growth." *The Bell Journal of Economics* 10 (Spring 1979): 92–116.

Griliches, Z. and Lichtenberg, F. "Interindustry Technology Flows and Productivity Growth: A Reexamination." *Review of Economics and Statistics* 66 (May 1984): 324–29.

_____. "R & D and Productivity Growth at the Industry Level: Is There Still a Relationship?" In *R & D, Patents, and Productivity,* edited by Z. Griliches, 465–501. Chicago: University of Chicago Press, 1984.

Gruber, W., Mehta, D. and Vernon, R. "The R and D Factor in International Trade and International Investment of United States Industries." *Journal of Political Economy* 75 (February 1967): 20–37.

Gruber, W. and Vernon, R. "The Technology Factor in the World Trade Matrix." In *The Technology Factor in International Trade,* edited by R. Vernon, 233–72. New York: National Bureau of Economic Research, 1970.

Hufbauer, G. "The Impact of National Characteristics and Technology on the Commodity Composition of Trade in Manufactured Goods." In *The Technology Factor in International Trade,* edited by R. Vernon, 145–231. New York: National Bureau of Economic Research, 1970.

Hymer, S. *The International Operations of National Firms: A Study of Direct Foreign Investment.* Cambridge: MIT Press, 1976.

Johnson, H. "Aspects of Patents and Licenses as Stimuli to Innovation." *Weltwirtschlaftliches Archiv* 112: 417–28.

Kamien, M. and Schwartz, N. "Market Structure and Innovation: A Survey." *Journal of Economic Literature* 13 (March 1975): 1–37.

Keesing, D. "The Impact of R and D on United States Trade." *Journal of Political Economy* 75 (February 1967): 38–48.

_____. "Labor Skills and Comparative Advantage." *American Economic Review* (p) 56 (May 1966): 249–58.

_____. "Labor Skills and International Trade: Evaluating Many Trade Flows With a Single Measuring Device." *Review of Economics and Statistics* 47 (August 1965): 287–94.

Kiechel, W. "The Decline of the Experience Curve." *Fortune* 104 (October 1981): 139–46.

Kindleberger, C., ed. *The International Corporation.* Boston: MIT Press, 1970.

Leontief, W. "Domestic Production and Foreign Trade, the American Capital Position Re-examined." In *AEA Readings in International Economics,* edited by R. Jones and H. Johnson, 503–27. Homewood, Ill.: Richard D. Irwin, 1968.

Lindert, P. and Kindleberger, C. *International Economics,* 7th ed. Homewood, Ill.: Richard D. Irwin, 1982.

Louis, A., "SmithKline Finds Rich Is Better." *Fortune* 102 (June 1980): 62–66.

Lustgarten, S. "Gains and Losses From Industrial Concentration: A Comment." *Journal of Law and Economics* 22 (April 1979): 183–90.

McGee, J. *In Defense of Industrial Concentration.* New York: Praeger, 1971.

Magee, S. "Application of the Dynamic Limit Pricing Model to the Price of Technology and International Transfer." In *Optimal Policies, Control Theory and Technology Exports,* edited by K. Brunner and A. Meltzer, 203–23. New York: North-Holland Publishing, 1977.

_____. "Information and the Multinational Corporation: An Appropriability Theory of Direct Foreign Investment." In *The New International Economic Order: The North-South Debate,* edited by J. Bhagwati, 317–43. Cambridge: MIT Press, 1977.

_____. "Multinational Corporations, the Industry Technology Cycle and Development." *Journal of World Trade Law* 11 (July/August 1977): 297–21.

Mansfield, E. "Technological Change and Market Structure." *American Economic Review* (p) 73 (May 1983): 205–9.

_____. "Composition of R and D Expenditures: Relationship to Size of Firm, Concentration, and Innovative Output." *Review of Economics and Statistics* 63 (November 1981): 610–15.

_____. *The Economics of Technological Change.* New York: W.W. Norton, 1968.

_____. *Industrial Research and Technological Innovation: An Econometric Analysis.* New York: W.W. Norton, 1968.

_____. "Industrial Research and Development Expenditures: Determinants, Prospects, and Relation to Size of Firm and Inventive Output." *Journal of Political Economy* 57 (August 1954): 319–40.

Mansfield, E., Romeo, A., Schwartz, M., Teece, D., Wagner, S., and Brach, P. *Technology Transfer, Productivity, and Economic Policy.* New York: W.W. Norton, 1982.

Mansfield, E., Romeo, A., and Wagner, S. "Foreign Trade and U.S. Research and Development." *Review of Economics and Statistics* 61 (February 1979): 49–57.

Markham, J. "Market Structure, Business Conduct and Innovation." *American Economic Review* (p) 55 (May 1966): 323–32.

National Industrial Conference Board. *Appraising Foreign Licensing Performance.* New York: National Industrial Conference Board, 1969.

National Science Foundation. *Research and Development in Industry 1973.* Washington: U.S. Government Printing Office, 1975.

Nelson, R. "Introduction." In *The Rate and Direction of Inventive Activity: Economic and Social Factors,* edited by R. Nelson, 3–16. Princeton: Princeton University Press, 1962.

Nelson, R., and Winter, S. "The Schumpeterian Tradeoff Revisited." *American Economic Review* 72 (March 1982): 114–32.

Office of Business Economics, U.S. Department of Commerce. *Input-Output Structure of the U.S. Economy: 1963.* Washington: U.S. Government Printing Office, 1969.

Peltzman, S. "The Causes and Consequences of Rising Concentration: A Reply." *Journal of Law and Economics* 22 (April 1979): 209–11.

_____. "The Gains and Losses From Industrial Concentration." *Journal of Law and Economics* 20 (October 1977): 229–63.

Peters, T. and Waterman, R. *In Search of Excellence.* New York: Harper & Row, 1982.

Robinson, R. "Factor Proportions and Comparative Advantage." In *AEA Readings in International Economics,* edited by R. Caves and H. Johnson, 3–23. Homewood, Ill.: Richard D. Irwin, 1968.

Rosenberg, N. *Perspectives on Technology.* New York: Cambridge University Press, 1976.

Salter, W. *Productivity and Technical Change.* Cambridge: Cambridge University Press, 1960.

Scherer, F. "Using Linked Patent and R & D Data to Measure Inter-industry Technology Flows." In *R & D, Patents, and Productivity,* edited by Z. Griliches, 417–64. Chicago: University of Chicago Press, 1984.

_____. "Inter-industry Technology Flows and Productivity Growth." *Review of Economics and Statistics* 64 (November 1982): 627–34.

_____. "The Causes and Consequences of Rising Industrial Concentration." *Journal of Law and Economics* 22 (April 1979): 191–208.

_____. *Industrial Market Structure and Economic Performance.* Chicago: Rand McNally, 1970.

_____. "Firm Size, Market Structure, Opportunity, and the Output of Patented Inventions." *American Economic Review* 55 (December 1965): 1097–1125.

Schumpeter, J. *Capitalism, Socialism, and Democracy.* New York: Harper & Row, 1950.

Shao, M. "Exxon's Mining Unit Finds It Tough Going After 16 Years in Field." *Wall Street Journal* (August 31, 1982).

Solow, R. "Technical Change and the Aggregate Production Function." *Review of Economics and Statistics* 39 (August 1957): 312–20.

Stigler, G. "The Division of Labor is Limited by the Extent of the Market." *Journal of Political Economy* 59 (June 1951): 185–93.

Stopford, J. and Wells, L. *Managing the Multinational Enterprise.* New York: Basic Books, 1972.

Strassman, P. *Technological Change and Economic Development.* Ithaca, N.Y.: Cornell University Press, 1968.

Teece, D. *The Multinational Corporation and the Resource Cost of International Technology Transfer.* Cambridge: Ballinger Publishing, 1976.

U.S. Bureau of the Census. *Census of Manufacturers, 1972.* Washington: U.S. Government Printing Office, 1975.

_____. *Census of Manufacturers, 1977.* Washington: U.S. Government Printing Office, 1980.

U.S. Department of Commerce. *Industry Profiles, 1958–1968.* Washington: U.S. Government Printing Office, 1970.

U.S. Department of Labor, Bureau of Labor Statistics. "Productivity Measures for Selected Industries, 1954–81." Bulletin 2155, December 1982. Washington: U.S. Government Printing Office.

_____. "Time Series Data for Input-Output Industries: Output, Prices, and Employment." Bulletin 2018, March 1979. Washington: U.S. Government Printing Office.

Vernon, R. *Storm Over the Multinationals.* Cambridge: Harvard University Press, 1977.

_____. *Sovereignty at Bay: The Multinational Spread of U.S. Enterprises.* New York: Basic Books, 1971.

_____. "International Investment and International Trade in the Product Cycle." *Quarterly Journal of Economics* 80 (May 1966): 190–207.

Waldolz, M. "Marketing Often is the Key to Success of Prescription Drugs." *Wall Street Journal* (December 28, 1981).

Weiss, L. "The Concentration-Profits Relationship and Antitrust." In *Industrial Concentration: The New Learning,* edited by H. Goldschmid, H. Mann, and J. Weston, 184–233. Boston: Little, Brown and Co., 1974.

Wells, L. "A Product Life Cycle for International Trade?" *Journal of Marketing* 32 (July 1968): 1–6.

Williams, J. "The Theory of International Trade Reconsidered." *Economic Journal* 39 (June 1929): 195–209.

Worley, J. "Industrial Research and the New Competition." *Journal of Political Economy* 59 (April 1961): 183–86.

Index

advertising, 61
appropriability theory (Magee), 3–6, 17–19, 36, 66, 69

Boston Consulting Group, 65
Brozen, Yale, 6, 45

capital goods industry, 13–14
"capital vintage" effect, 67
Census of Manufacturers, 46, 52
Cobb-Douglas production function, 74
collusion, 6–7, 45, 49, 55, 85
concentration. *See* industry concentration
Conference Board, 33, 34
consumer goods industries, 58, 85
control theory, 24

Demsetz' hypothesis, 6–7, 70, 78, 83, 86. *See also* efficiency; industry concentration; market structure
differential cost efficiency hypothesis, 85

economies of scale, 64–67, 83, 85, 86. *See also* firm size; market structure
efficiency, 7, 46, 55; "best practice" technique, 57, 67; managerial, 66, 85. *See also* Demsetz' hypothesis; profitability
entrepreneurship, 12, 14–15, 16, 21, 36
"experience curve" strategies, 65–66, 95n43

firm size, 32, 49; growth rates and, 67; R and D and, 12, 18, 26, 38, 40, 43; research personnel and, 40–41. *See also* economies of scale; market structure
foreign trade. *See* international trade

Gaskin's dynamic limit pricing model, 24–25
Griliches, Zvi, 70, 75

Hecksher-Ohlin factor proportions theory of trade, 1–2, 9, 14, 91n3

industry age, 25–26
industry concentration: appropriability costs and, 18; changes in, 55–68; industry unit costs and, 7, 49, 65, 70; productivity and, 28, 70; profits and, 45–46; rates of return and, 47–49; R and D and, 32, 38, 70–83. *See also* Demsetz' hypothesis; market structure; "natural oligopoly" theory (Peltzman)
industry costs, 56–57
industry technology cycle theory (Magee), 16–20, 24–32, 36, 69
innovation, 3–4; labor-saving, 21; material-saving, 21; process, 7, 21, 78, 85; product, 4, 21, 85, 86. *See also* product development; research and development (R and D); technological change
international trade: R and D and, 1–2, 4, 9–16, 20; technology transfer and, 5–6; theory of, 1, 7. *See also* Hecksher-Ohlin factor proportions theory of trade; multinational corporations (MNCs); product cycle theory of trade and investment (Vernon)
investment: domestic, 12; foreign, 5–6, 12; private, 16–17, 56, 61, 69, 70. *See also* multinational corporations (MNCs); product cycle theory of trade and investment (Vernon)

joint venture, 34. *See also* technology transfer

Leontief paradox, 9, 92n3
less developed countries (LDCs), locating production facilities in, 16
licensing, 33–34. *See also* technology transfer
Line of Business survey (FTC), 28, 75, 76